LIVE THE LIFE OF EXCELLENCE

MATT TREPPEL

Mallory —
keep striving in His Excellence

Matt

ISBN: 978-1-935256-08-3

Published by L'Edge Press
A ministry of Upside Down Ministries, Inc.
PO Box 2567
Boone, NC 28607

ACKNOWLEDGEMENTS

I dedicate this book to my wife Marlies. May I show our girls – Arianna, Lilli and Gloria how much I love them by demonstrating my love for you.

Thank you, Father

Special thanks for those who were willing to share:
Jimmy Joe Sintic
Kim DiBiase
Julie Thompson
Marlies Treppel

Jeff Hendley, L'Edge Press

Abbie Frease, Graphic Designer

Table Of Contents

Introduction

"See George, you really did have a wonderful life." Clarence wanted so desperately to earn his wings. Other angels started "talking." It had been 400 plus years that he has been in heaven and this was his biggest opportunity yet. In the movie *It's a Wonderful Life* Clarence is assigned to go to Earth and help out a very discouraged and desperate man named George Bailey. George is married with children and owns a small town savings and loan. When the company runs into trouble and everything looks bleak all difficulties around George are magnified in his mind and he is only left with the conclusion that everyone would be better off if he never existed. Clarence gives George the great gift of seeing just how everyone in his life would be affected if George never was born. What transpires is an incredible revelation of so many small decisions and seemingly inconsequential actions that have such a profound affect not only on individuals in his life but also indirectly to others who are in those individuals life years down the road. It basically is a domino effect.

George is so shook up and saddened about all that has happened he begs Clarence for his life back. The life that he thought messed up so many others lives. The life that he felt failed himself, his wife, his children and so many others, was a wonderful life. George got his life back and was never going to be the same. It was Christmas Eve and everyone came to George's house when news went around town that he was in trouble. All those people that he felt he had done nothing but cause trouble for were on their way to his house to be there for him for all that he has done for them. They cared. George has had such an impact on their lives. He was a positive impact on their lives. He would never have known if he went ahead and took his own life. Ironically, as George contemplated jumping off a bridge into the icy water below to end his life he jumped in to save a life; Clarence's. Clarence jumped in to save George's life. Clarence knew the heart that George had. He knew that he was selfless and other people focused.

Clarence knew that it meant more to George that someone else is lifted up even if it meant he had to stay down. Most importantly, Clarence knew that the most valuable thing is life itself. George had such huge dreams for his own life. He didn't have time to get married or even to stay in that little town. He was going to travel the world. Explore it times over. He was going to build huge buildings and be a front runner in industry. George, as a preteen, had his whole life mapped out. Only thing though is that God had a different plan and allowed George to get to a place of brokenness. At that place of despair and exhaustion does one have their eyes opened to God's amazing grace. For George it was a whole lot of his town folk coming to his rescue. When everyone heard that George was in trouble they stopped what they were doing and went to his house to financially help him. But also to remind him of all that he had done for them and that they wouldn't know where they would be without him. The things that people said were the same as when Clarence took him around the town to show him everything that transpired if he wasn't born. He finally understood what they knew. He was important to them. He was meaningful in their lives and they so much appreciated him. He was a blessing to them and he thought he had become a curse. When we allow the truth to shine through we can truly see that we have been given a wonderful life. How we respond to God's will for our lives is what makes it truly remarkable. Unfortunately so many people don't get that same opportunity to see how valuable their life is and they go through life just getting by one day to the next wishing it was some other way. George wished his life was another way but got to see that the way he was living wasn't inconsequential. It was wonderful because he blessed so many people. It was wonderful because he lived his life serving others and sacrificing so that others could have. He lived a life of excellence.

Live a life of excellence? I felt anything but that in the early fall of 2009. I sat in my car outside the Holiday Inn at a beach resort. Midweek; mid morning. I was asked to speak at a luncheon for a corporate function being held at the hotel. Here I am trying to gain my focus on what I am to be speaking on and instead I am burdened down with difficulties of business. With the economy in a recession the business that my wife and I own has been under great financial stress. We had fallen behind greatly in paying our bills and we ran out of avenues to gain capital. We had incredible challenges with the banks, customers and vendors. I felt much was to my blame even with the recession. I was questioning decisions I had made. I was inconsistent in the specifics I was responsible for that our employees needed from me for them to complete their jobs efficiently. I didn't feel

I was doing a good job in leading our company. I was doing more personal training; having more opportunities to speak and working with college athletes and coaches with the Fellowship of Christian Athletes. These are my passions that I desire to be full time one day. But, right now, am I doing it at the expense of our business?

So, why am I here? I closed my eyes, paused and prayed. In spite of all that was going on in my business life how was I living my life? We can get so fixed on one aspect of our life; especially work and we let that define us and dictate everything else. If someone walked into a room that you were in and they had a pen in their shirt pocket that had exploded, and there was a big ink spot on it, your focus would be on nothing but the spot. If someone were to ask you to identify him you most likely say," The sad sap with the exploded pen in their shirt pocket." You might choose to substitute sad sap with fool, loser or clown. The man's suit might be very impressive in every other detail. It might be a tailored Armani with exquisite cufflinks. Everything is pressed and clean except 2% of the whole outfit; the perfectly pressed white collared shirt with the ink stained pocket. We would focus on that 2% and neglect to see the very impressive 98%. That 2% is what we might mention about this person to our spouse when we got home. In *It's a Wonderful Life* George Bailey believes his life is a failure because of the poor financial condition of his business. He allowed that to be his barometer of everything else. No, in spite of that, he lived his life impeccably and always serving and encouraging others. In the end he realized that he was living a life of excellence.

I wasn't at this convention to tell successful business people how to be successful business people. I was there to challenge and encourage them outside of business to live abundant and fruitful lives. I was there to inspire them to live an abundant life; a life of excellence, regardless of how successful or unsuccessful they may be. I wasn't there to talk about how to grow the bottom line of the P & L. After all I just told you that would seem quite foolish and a bit ironic. No, just as I felt unqualified to write my first book it was the same for all of the speaking I was doing. It isn't about me. It's about what God is doing in and through me to live perseveringly and faithfully towards God's standards in spite of circumstances and situations. It is not about being delivered from adversities, but being strong in the midst of them. The question that came back to me in my prayer was how was I living my life amid all the circumstances surrounding me?

This book isn't about me telling you all that I have accomplished and you should do as I do and you too will live a life of excellence. A lot of what I am sharing in this book is what I have been led to in order to improve in my life. I have been inspired by others, challenged; to strive higher than where I have settled at. Some are things that God has opened my eyes to that I need to add or delete from my life to be more of whom He has called me to be. But each is works in progress at different stages. I am inviting you along on the journey with me as I seek to incorporate different aspects of this book into my life that I may be a better tool for God. In doing so I would be a better friend; a better father and husband. It is harder to step out and do when everything around you seems to be struggling. But that is exactly what this world needs; to see individuals stepping up in tough times. We live in tough times. Change doesn't come from a slogan or motto. Change comes when individuals decide to make change in their lives that have a positive effect on those around them.

The challenge, the opportunity, is for us to fulfill the potential of the God given abilities and gifts within us that would be an inspiration to others. It is to live a life of excellence.

CHAPTER I

PREDESTINATION; IT'S YOUR CHOICE

"After the death of Moses the servant of the
Lord, it came to pass that the Lord spoke
to Joshua the son of Nun, Moses assistant,
saying: "Moses My servant is dead. Now
therefore, arise, go over this Jordan, you
and all this people, to the land which I am
giving them—the children of Israel. Every
place that the sole of your foot will tread
upon I have given you, as I said to Moses.
From the wilderness and this Lebanon as
far as the great river, the River Euphrates,
all the land of the Hittites, and to the Great
Sea toward the going down of the sun,
shall be your territory. No man shall be
able to stand before you all the days of your
life; as I was with Moses, so I will be with
you. I will not leave you nor forsake you.
Be strong and of good courage, for to this
people you shall divide as an inheritance
the land which I swore to their fathers
to give them. Only be strong and very
courageous, that you may observe to do
according to all the law which Moses My
servant commanded you; do not turn from

it to the right hand or to the left, that you may prosper wherever you go. This Book of the Law shall not depart from your mouth, but you shall meditate in it day and night, that you may observe to do according to all that is written in it. For then you will make your way prosperous, and then you will have good success. Have I not commanded you? Be strong and of good courage; do not be afraid, nor be dismayed, for the Lord your God is with you wherever you go.'"
– Joshua 1:1-9

I find this passage intriguing; fascinating. God has a will and a purpose for His designated people. He tells Joshua that the time is now. It is time for him to lead the Israelites into the promised land. This was a promise of a land that was first foretold to Abraham hundreds of years earlier. God had a faithful and obedient man in Joshua who was a warrior; trusted by the people to guide and lead them by God's command. What I find that is interesting is that God tells Joshua some guaranteed facts; that they will attain a specific piece of land and that no one will be able to thwart Joshua. However, after stating this, God tells Joshua that there are certain things he must be obedient to do in order for these specifics to occur. And that he must not be afraid and that he need be strong and courageous. Guaranteed victory but it appears to be with a condition. He wants Joshua to understand that He must trust what God says and that His "guarantee's" are guaranteed if Joshua does what God commands him to do and that it will be tough and challenging. God wants Joshua to understand that it is only possible by God. This will of God can only come about by God, not by Joshua. If it is going to be by God, than it must be God's way.

As I have read, studied, memorized, internalized and meditated on this scripture I have come to see that it applies to myself. It is that God has a plan that He has predestined for my life; it is, though, of my own choosing.

> "'For I know the plans I have for you,' declares the Lord, 'plans to prosper you and not to harm you, plans to give you hope and a future.'" – Jeremiah 29:11 NIV

There has been much talk, debate and discussion about "predestination" over the centuries. If God already knows what you are going to do than you have no control and you can do just nothing. That no matter what you do or do not do it already has been predetermined and therefore you are just a robot living out what has already been set. A good point that has been made is that if God already knows everything and can see all time from the beginning from the end then we really don't have a choice in what we do or say for it already has been established. It can give you a headache. Well, it is time for me to chime in on my belief. The answer to both sides of the argument? Yes, you are right. Yes your life is predetermined. And, yes, you choose with your own free will. Here, let me explain. My truth comes from the Bible which I believe of what it says of itself that it is inerrant; without fallacy. The Bible says that God's will, which He has predetermined for people, or all people, doesn't always happen. A case in point is salvation. In 2 Peter 3:9 we are told that God doesn't "will" anyone to perish. Perish defined as being eternally separated from God. God has reconciled sinning man to Himself through the sacrificial lamb, His son, Jesus. In the book of Roman's we are told that "for all have sinned and fall short of the glory of God." And that "sin leads to death" but "that if you confess with your mouth the Lord Jesus and believe in your heart that God raised Him from the dead, you will be saved. For with the heart one believes unto righteousness, and with the mouth confession is made unto salvation." – Romans 3:23, 6:23, 10:9-10. According to the Bible God wants everyone to spend eternity with Him after their physical life on Earth ends. These scriptures that I quote are His way of redeeming sinful people back to Himself. God says He is holy and nothing unholy can be in His presence. The only way for us to be holy in God's presence is that we have someone who takes all our sins upon themselves that we are no longer unholy. We have that one person in Jesus. "For He made Him who knew no sin to be sin for us, that we might become the righteousness of God in Him." – 2 Corinthians 5:21. He wills and desires for every single person to be with Him forever. It is accepting Jesus as our substitute, He died for our sins, and we are made right with God. "Therefore, having been justified by faith, we have peace with God through our Lord Jesus Christ, through whom also we have access by faith into this grace in which we stand, and rejoice in hope of the glory of God." – Romans 5:1

Do you believe all that I wrote in the last paragraph? Not everyone does. Some people don't believe it to be true. Others believe that it is only one way but there are many other ways. Jesus says," I am the way, the truth, and the life. No one comes to the Father except through Me." – John 14:6. Some do not believe in a god and certainly not the God of the Bible. I believe, more than what is right in front of my face, that God is and is who He says He is and that His living Word is truth. I believe His way is the only way. But not everyone does. Therefore, according to the Bible, though God's will is for all to believe, God's will, will not come to fruition. There are many who have and many who will reject it. The Bible also states that truth.

God's will was also that He would be the people of Israel's King. His will was not for them to have a human king like the other nation's. However, they pressed on demanding Samuel that they wanted a king out of the people. God's will didn't prevail and Israel got what they wanted.

How powerful it seems that we can choose to accept what God has planned for each of us individually or we can choose to follow our own path. As I have meditated on the Joshua text I question at first how can Joshua do anything but what God has promised him. Guaranteed victory and would seem to give Joshua incredible confidence in that no one would be able to stand before him. He would be top dog. But, what circumstance or situation would bring him to a place of fear? And not only did God call on him to be courageous once but a second time and that was to be "very" courageous. What does that imply?

God has a plan for my life and it's good. Is it better than what I want to do for my life?

I believe He has a plan for us that first and foremost that our life glorifies Him. In that our words, actions and decisions would be to sow life into others; to reap good fruit in this world. They would reflect a gracious loving Creator. I believe, just as with Joshua, there are many things in this world that would have us "turn to the right hand or the left" and would get us off the track that God would have us follow. He has created us. He knows each of us mentally, physically, spiritually, physiologically, psychologically. (Maybe some other ogically's.) He knows the deepest recesses of our being and knows what would hinder, hurt, and pain us. He knows us better than we know ourselves. So then, why do I choose to do or say contrary to what He would have for me to do? If I believe all that I have wrote proceeding this then why would I be disobedient? Plainly, why would I still sin? I know I do, I turn to the right hand and the left. In this day and age those things that are to the right hand or the left hand are a million different distractions that can bring us to a belief that there is much more satisfying options in the world than what God would present to us. I have allowed the things that are important in the world become important to me. Just as Joshua was instructed to focus on God and His commands and His ways so that he and the people of Israel would be distinctly different from the peoples surrounding where they are so am I to be likewise consecrated.

We put more attention, thought, debate into who is going to win American Idol and argue about who should or shouldn't of been voted off the island than we are about atrocities that are being committed in this world to others. We pay more respect and give homage to a celebrity or athlete than we will to an expert in a certain field. We spend incredible amounts of money on video games and electronic do-da's than on investing in the education of our children. And why? Because we have conformed to the world's priorities. Individuals will spend countless hours working on their fantasy football league, more than they will spend time with their children or their spouse. It is a good thing that television needed electricity to be invented or Thomas Edison would of spent his time watching countless hours of television instead of being occupied with inventing the light bulb. Of course he would be watching it in the dark. God's plans for our lives have been pushed aside by the world's plan. How much time do you spend on Facebook? Texting? Internet surfing? TV surfing? How much time do you seek knowing God and His will and desire for your life? How much quicker would this book of been written if I didn't just "see" what's on TV first? I do believe that I am missing out on what God would have for me. What He would have for me is the most fulfilling anything in life could offer; most sustaining and complete.

What compounds this is that in all this we get off track of what is important. In the movie Field of Dreams one of the characters is Archie Graham. Archie has always dreamed of being a professional baseball player back in the first half of the 20th century and his focus and time was spent on sharpening his skills to give himself the best chance he could in realizing that dream. He only got called up to the majors for one game and only was a late inning replacement and didn't have one official at bat. He was sent back to the minors and soon was out of baseball. Later on in his twilight years, Archie, played by Burt Lancaster, was known as Moonlight Graham and was a small town doctor. But with the help of Kevin Costner's character he can go back to being that young man and stay and play baseball forever. He reminisced with nostalgia the feel and the smells of the game and how he loved them so. Ray (Kevin Costner) was all giddy to get him back and to live out that dream forever. Dr. Graham turned him down. Ray was besides himself. So many people would jump at the chance to be a pro player. Ray said it would be a shame if he didn't take him up on it. The first time I saw the movie I am thinking the same thing. Shoot! What a young American boy wouldn't do to be a pro player. He said that most people would say it would be a shame to have only been a pro player for just one day. I remember the first time that I heard the response from Doc Graham and thinking how right he is and how wrong Ray and myself were. How easily our priorities get muddled and clouded. How we allow unimportant things overtake that which is truly important. This was Doc Graham's answer. "No, it would have been a shame if I had only been a doctor for one day." How did we miss that? Of course that is more important. Sometimes we need someone or something else to sober us up to truth.

So what things to the right hand and to the left that I have turned to that have distracted me from focusing on the substance of God's intentions for me? If you watch enough television, read enough magazines and listen to enough radio (we all get more than enough) we are being brainwashed by advertisers and programs to what they would have us to believe that is important for us. Trying to convince us that in consumption of things; whether foods, clothing, games, movies, etc, will give us fulfillment. I recently saw a commercial for Direct TV. In general its slogan was just like everyone else's. "Direct TV will change your life." All this stuff will change your life. And boy do we fall for it.

God knew that Joshua and the people, in their humanity, would fall to the ways of the people that lived around the promised land. God knew that the customs and beliefs of these people were not of God and therefore would be detrimental to them. God knew that in order for Joshua and the people to carry out His will for them they would have to be focused and leave aside those things that would keep them from realizing what God had predestined for them. Just a little of the distractions will create an appetite for more and soon those things become priority and what God would have us do to grow us into His will we would do after all the other "stuff" was done. One study says that in one day walking in Manhattan a individual will be exposed to over 7,000 advertisements. Hypnotized, is more like it. I spoke in my first book *Live the Life Abundant* that I would watch my television programs; you know the make believe stuff with characters and a script, and when they were done I would spend a few minutes reading and praying as I fell asleep. I allowed the things of the world, the distractions, to take precedence over the creator of all that was real. It was only after I chose to put aside that regiment each night and seek Him first did I begin to grow and discover the gifts and talents that He had given to me and start using me in ministry for Him. Once I put my focus on Him He put His focus into me. I praise God everyday for that patience He had for me and His unrelenting pursuit for me to seek His predestined plan for my life over the worldly one's that I was following. One's that didn't bring any fulfillment but quick bursts of escape that didn't hold much substance or quench the internal thirst we all have. I had to consciously choose, daily, to focus on Him and close my eyes and ears as much as possible to all the junk around me.

> "…let us lay aside every weight, and the sin which so easily ensnares us, and let us run with endurance the race that is set before us, looking unto Jesus, the author and finisher of our faith, who for the joy that was set before Him endured the cross, despising shame, and sat down at the right hand of God." – Hebrews 12: 1b-2

Weights do not necessarily have to be bad things. They could very well be godly things. But, they very well could be godly things that God hasn't called you to do. Sometimes we have good intentions but end up getting in God's way. Sometimes we feel we want to be someone God hasn't desired for us to be. I believe that there are pastors in the pulpit that want to be pastors but God hasn't anointed to be. Weights can be the cares of this world that we burden ourselves with that we weren't called to. We don't see God taking care of something, or in the way we feel it should go, so we intercede. At church we don't see someone stepping up to do something we feel needs to be done. We aren't trusting God so we decide to shoulder the burden ourselves. "God is more pleased with the least bit of obedience than all the services you think of rendering Him" – John of the Cross. There can be too many extracurricular activities that take away from the focus on the more important aspects of our lives.

That leads me to what I believe is what most leads a person adrift from the life that God has predestined for them.

> "The thief does not come except to steal,
> and to kill, and to destroy. I have come
> that they may have life, and that they may
> have it more abundantly." – John 10:10

This scripture was the crux of my first book *Live the Life Abundant*. The enemy, Satan, is called by Jesus, the father of lies and that there is no truth in him. Just as he manipulated and deceived Eve he still does this to this day to those who are focused on things of this world. In Paul's letter to the Romans he compels us to "not conform to this world, but be transformed by the renewing of your mind, that you may prove what is that good and acceptable and perfect will of God." – Romans 12:2. Satan has free reign on the earth. He gets our mind onto things of the flesh. We spend our time, money and drive onto getting wealth. The drive leads to greed. Today so many young people (and probably many older people as well) are fixated on being on reality TV. They want to be seen, want to be known. Too many parents have their children traveling all year long playing sports at the expense of everything else. As Doc Graham said," It would be a shame if he only was a doctor for one day instead of being a baseball player." Many today might say they agree but their actions and decisions say otherwise. We spend so much time and money thinking that those things we do and consume will bring fulfillment. We neglect and diminish the importance of real life shaping focus. What the enemy destroys is our ambition and desire to do the concrete hard life changing things. Instead of studying or learning to do something that can be meaningful we get distracted and watch another movie on one of the 35 movie channels on our cable or decide to play one more game, which stretches to 10 more, on our Xbox. Even perhaps we spend the time, money and energy getting and hooking up our DirectTV; because it "will change our life." In all of this distraction we lose sight of what will truly satisfy our inner desires; God's will for us. That might be harder and surely not as fun. It will cost us some free time but we will grow more into who God has called us to be instead of what the enemy would have us settle to be; sound and fury signifying nothing. Doing a whole lot of nothing achieving nothing. But, if we seek to do what has substance we can improve our lives and have a impact on improving the world around us. This leads to the abundant life that God wants us to experience and live and the life that the enemy wants to steal, kill and destroy.

So how do we combat that?

> "But seek first the kingdom of God and His righteousness, and all these things shall be added to you." – Matthew 6:33

We must be deliberate in giving each day to God at the very onset of that day.

> "You have to get up every morning with determination if you're going to go to bed with satisfaction." – George Horace Lorimer. We must ask God for wisdom and clarity, every single day, to what that satisfaction is. We must acknowledge that we do have an enemy who would have us be ineffective in having a life of excellence and in turn being a motivation for others. We need to understand that we have to be on guard of how easily it is for us to slip away from His purpose and go with the flow. As I stated in the beginning of this chapter it will take

individuals working hard with determination that will be a catalyst for others to do the same to change the mind-set of our country. If we deliberately make this a habit we will transform our own personal mind-set that will allow us to avoid and ignore the superficial things that beg for our attention and stay on the path of God's daily will for us. As we grow in this transformation we will more and more be able to lay aside the weights, distractions and sins and not easily be persuaded to turn to the right hand or the left "that you may prosper wherever you go."

In order for us to be successful in putting aside the ways of the world and attain God's predestined will for our lives we must be obedient to His word. And it is His word that is more powerful than anything else in all creation.

> "For the word of God is living and powerful, and sharper than any two edge sword, piercing even to the division of soul and spirit, and of joint and marrow, and is a discerner of the thoughts and intents of the heart." – Hebrews 4:12

In this scripture we are told of the penetrating power of the word of God into our entire personal being; mind, body and spirit. All that you are, everything, 100%! Nothing is missed. We are told in the first chapter of John's gospel that Jesus is that word. It is He who penetrates and knows all of you. It is when you surrender to Him that He will orchestrate God's will into your heart. We must take the word and make it a priority in our lives. There is a direct correlation in the absorbing of the word and prosperity. It is God's Prosperity on the inside that overflows our cup and is a blessing to others. Satan certainly doesn't want you to allow the word of God to be a priority in your life. He knows it is a truth that he has no power against. Most people do not know the incredible life transcending power of the living word of God. If satan is able to distract you with all the fluff, all the pudding, of this world you won't have time and will not build up a discipline to be in the word. In His word comes the ability to attain His will. Joshua was told of this very important, essential ingredient in his life for God's will for the people of Israel to be accomplished.

> "This Book of the Law shall not depart from your mouth, but you shall meditate in it day and night, that you may observe to do according to all that is written in it. For then you will make your way prosperous, and then you will have good success."
> – Joshua 1:8

For me, this one verse is vital in the manifestation of God's predestined will for our lives. Joshua's obedience to this command is of great consequence for the entire Hebrew people. How crucially significant is it for each of us? How will our obedience or disobedience to this command and subsequent promise have an ineradicable affect on our spouse and children?

How much of God's will is never culminated?

How about in your life?

CHAPTER 2

3 Ring Circus

Father God, I am clay in your hands
Help me stay that way through all life's demands
'Cause they chip and they nag and they pull at me
And every little thing I make up my mind to be
Like I'm gonna be a daddy who's in the mix
And I'm gonna be a husband who stays legit
And I pray that I'm an artist who rises above the road
That is wide and filled with self love
Everything that I see draws me
Though it's only in You that I can truly see
That it's a feast for the eyes – a low blow to purpose
And I am a little kid at a three ring circus

A little rap by Toby Mac – from "Lose My Soul"

It has been over thirty years but I can remember it clearly. We took the train to Penn Station which has a stop underneath Madison Square Garden. It was the first of many trips to the Garden and most memorable. We went into the Garden and it…was…AWESOME. Wow; Ringling Brothers and Barnum Bailey Circus. There was so much going on; the color, the brightness; the clowns on unicycles, elephants. Guy on stilts, 20 foot in the air, juggling. Tigers jumping thru hoops. Overstimulation

I am sure, but for a 7-8 year old it was exhilarating. My head was on a swivel. There just isn't enough time to soak everything in. Once you started focusing on something that was the coolest thing – bam! There would be something even cooler. There was nothing like it. Then you leave and your mind is on overdrive. Everything I saw flashing in and out of my thoughts. Adrenaline kicking!

A little kid at a three ring circus.

A little kid at a three ring circus with all the sights and sounds is fun. Now as an adult there seem to be even more sights and sounds trying to lure us away from the best intentions. I think about each day. I start in the dark, early in the morning. Everyone is asleep. It is dark outside, early morning. It's pure quiet. I go in my closet and begin my day by surrendering it to God; seeking His will as a husband, father, friend, employer. But, first and foremost, it is as an obedient follower of Christ. I want, desire, to focus on the things that He would have me to do. The things I need to do. The person I need to be. In that quiet time I am able to focus. I get up and get the day going with my family and as I walk out the door life meets me. Life can be a 3 ring circus. Good and bad. And throughout the day we can lose our focus, our attention. Our 5 senses might lead us this way or another. I know for me, I can easily start doing one thing, drift to another, lose my attention and start doing something else. Instead of reading I might first watch a little of the game. Don't like commercials so I start flipping around. Talk about a 3 ring circus. That's the tube. It fills your head with junk. It is not only the TV but also the radio. It can even be listening to Christian music. Sometimes, a lot of the time, we need to shut it off. We text, email, facebook, twitter and speak on our cell phone. We go in so many directions and go nowhere. And what was our original purpose? Love, serve and contribute? The Apostle Paul tells us that we have a continual war inside of us, spirit of God and our natural man spirit. One is focused on turning away from the things of this world and to God and one to satisfy all our flesh appetites.

Back in the day, way back, when someone went to the store they went for a specific purpose, specific items to buy. They went to the counter, told the sales clerk what it is that they would like and he/she would go in the back and get it. You know what you needed and it was gotten for you. You were in control. Now you go to the store and, just like a circus, there is so much that lures you. Aisles and aisles of you name it. We have been dumbed down to believe that the marketing giants of Madison Avenue know better than ourselves what it is that we want; and what we think we want will make us happy and satisfied. We have allowed ourselves to be controlled in so many ways by visual aids from TV to magazines to billboards to radio commercials. It is horribly wrong that persons can be trampled to death at the opening of a store that has the newest of the fad dolls or games. That someone is in the line to get in is an example of the media telling them what they absolutely have to get, indirectly through their children. We know, they know, that in a few months that this prized possession will go from must have or can't live; to just another toy/ game that had lost its luster and put aside because the next best new thing is coming available. As I write this exact sentence it is March 15, 2010. Not just yet 3 months since Christmas came and went. The other day my girls were telling me how bored they were. My mind went back to Christmas when there were a plethora of new toys and games. Each of my 3 girls received from Santa to Mom and Dad; grandparents and aunts, more than enough. They were so excited but almost worried that they wouldn't find enough time to truly devote reasonable time to each. Where to start? What a challenge they had on their hands! When we were shopping we had to get such and such because if we didn't our children would be the laughingstock of their school and they would be scarred for life. Not to mention that they would probably never forgive us.

Living a life of excellence is living a life under control.

> "Only be strong and very courageous, that
> you observe to do according to all the law
> which Moses My servant commanded you;
> do not turn from it to the right hand or
> to the left, that you may prosper wherever
> you go." – Joshua 1:7

The first nine verses of Joshua, chapter 1, is one of my favorite slices of the Bible. Joshua has been obedient and patient as well as loyal to Moses. After the death of Moses God calls Joshua to lead the people into the Promised Land that God had promised long ago through Abraham. God tells Joshua exactly what He wants Him to do and precisely where the boundaries of their land will stretch to. He tells Joshua that no one will be able to thwart him. Here is God; The Almighty creator and sovereign ruler over all creation telling Joshua a matter of fact. So it's a done deal, right? This is what my answer to the argument of predestination. Yes, your life is predestined. However, it is your choice. Huh? Oxymoron? God's will for Joshua and the people of Israel was laid out; however Joshua was going to have to choose obedience in order for God's will to become reality. God lays out what will definitely be for the people if they do as He wishes. God tells Joshua here in verse 7 what is going to be needed to be done because God knows what can distract Joshua and the people. He knows what it is around them that will lure them away from what God's best for them would be. What was it that would be around Joshua that would get him off the focus of leading the people to set down where God had called them to be? "Do not turn from it to the left hand or to the left..." Think about when you have a task at hand and you're able to block out everything and focus and accomplish the agenda you set out to accomplish. Sometimes we have to get away from the crowd, even sometimes our family. We turn off the TV, radio; put our phone on "quiet", because we know that it is crucial that the task needs our undivided attention. That it is going to take all that is within us to achieve. Isn't that why your mom/dad wouldn't let you do your homework in front of the television? You wouldn't be able to do as well as you could do if you weren't being distracted. No matter how much you pleaded that it wouldn't. That is what God sees with Joshua and the Israelites. He knows that the people living around the area that they are going to be at will have attractive lifestyles that are contradictive to the life that God wants them to lead. Those other peoples will seem to be having a whole lot of fun over there. How about when you are bound and determined to get something accomplished and you are making headway and a friend or friends stop over and try to convince you to go with them. "Let's Go and have so much fun, we never get to hang out that much anymore."

"It's a perfect day for it." "Come on, you can do that work some other time." "They are treating!" You turn to the right or the left and your drive to complete the mission has been subjugated. You think that it will be no big deal to pick up where you left off later. And you don't. Other stuff and things take our mind to other places and away from our original desire. We are drawn and ensnared by our feelings and emotions that pull us away to sights and sounds all around us. We need to see what is going on. We need to partake for if we miss out on the events surrounding us, we feel we are missing something where in reality we are missing out on God's will and plan for us; which is the fulfillment of satisfaction for our very being.

I am going to tell you the story of two guys that I know who played football in the NFL. One, I will not use his real name but will call him Josh, played his college ball at a national power. Josh had a very successful college career and was drafted into the NFL where he quickly became a starter before his first game. The other one, who I will use his real name, Jim Kitts, played at a smaller, Division III school. Jim had a successful college career as well; however it is very hard to get an opportunity to play in the NFL from the Division III level. Jim had to first make headway in lower profession football ranks. It was very hard at the onset but he never doubted that he would play in the NFL. He would do everything he possibly could knowing that if he didn't make it he gave it his all. Initially, it was very difficult and almost gave up in just getting on the roster with an Arena Football League team. He put on the blinders, focused, persevered and had a great year. Jim was then given the opportunity to play in the NFL. He played multiple years having the experience of playing with both Dan Marino and Brett Favre. Josh, who I told you won the starting job at his position before his first game, was cut by the team before the season had ever ended. That team reached the Super Bowl that year. Josh didn't play again in the NFL. A former NFL player, who played for the same team Josh played for, said that Josh got caught up in the nightlife of the big city. Josh was given a signing bonus and nice contract that enabled him to buy things, do things; which became a distraction. Josh got immersed in the three ring circus. Jim had the discipline to use all his resources that enabled him to play in the NFL. Josh used all distractions of the three ring circus to curtail his great opportunity of an NFL career. In talking with Jim, the most decisive choice that was most integral in him succeeding and realizing his dream of playing professional football was laying aside all the "stuff" that can take away your time and focus. He was focused on fulfilling his dream and made a choice to avoid and ignore that which would deter him.

Discipline is the key. In the book *Spiritual Disciplines For The Christian Life*, Donald S. Whitney tells a great story about what I alluded to earlier "Predestination – It's your choice."

The story, paraphrased, tells of a boy that has guitar lessons every week that his parents are making him take. During the week he has time set aside each day to sit and go over practicing the lesson that was given to him by his teacher, which he meets with every week. The boy would sit down to begin practice, which he loathed, when he would hear the neighborhood kids outside playing. He would begrudgingly go away from the window and pick up his guitar and practice. He would get frustrated for he felt clumsy with the instrument in his hands and was having a rough time trying to figure out the notes in front of him. He would have a hard time trying to remember where his fingers would go on the strings. As he fumbled a bit the sound wasn't exactly smooth and enjoyable. And because of that he didn't enjoy it at all. The boy practiced out of duty and surely would put up the guitar for good if it would ever become voluntary. Well, one day the boy was sitting down passing the practice time by when suddenly appeared an angel. This angel whisked the boy away. With just a snap of his fingers the angel had the boy looking down at Carnegie Hall. A big audience marveled as a guitar virtuoso strummed the guitar in such a smooth style. His fingers were dancing on the strings with fluidity and grace; with such ease. The man playing the guitar was in such rhythm and harmony. It was as if he and the guitar were one. He had such joy on his face. The boy never heard such awesome music, especially not from the noise that he made. The boy just sat there stunned at how awesome it was. The angel asked him if he liked it. The boy in stunned bewilderment just nodded his head with his mouth agape. The angel said "good" because that man is you in 20 years. And just like that the boy was back in his living room with his bulky guitar. The angel said "now practice" and was gone.

Oh gosh. How many times? How many times have you said, "Tomorrow, yes, I will start tomorrow." This procrastination is a crippler in us realizing our potential; accomplishing our goals.

We get a glimpse of what our discipline and focus can bring us. We get excited about it and wake up the next day with pure intentions of acting on it. Finally, we have direction to the desires within. But first we have other things we need to do; like going to work. Work is done and we are tired so we will veg on the couch first. Find a movie or the game and 2 hours later you are even more tired and have lost the ambition. What the "it" is, isn't really important. For each of us it is something different. It could be exercising, reading a book, writing a book, taking online classes, taking karate class, volunteering at the senior center, learning to play the guitar! In each of these we can have an epiphany and it all looks great in our mind. However with anything we are going to have to sacrifice something else. Usually, that something else is pudding. Pudding? Yes, pudding. Pudding tastes good but has no nutritional value and won't fill you up. Oh, but it sure tastes good even if it doesn't last a minute.

"Therefore we also, since we are surrounded by so great a cloud of witnesses, let us lay aside every weight, and the sin which so easily ensnares us, and let us run with endurance the race that is set before us, looking unto Jesus, the author and finisher of our faith." – Hebrews 12:1-2a

Work, paycheck, pay bills.

CNN, CNNSI, NBC, CNBC, MSNBC, ESPN, ESPN2, ESPN360, ESPNU, ESPNC, ESPNN, ESPND, ESPN3, HBO, HBO-E, HBO2, HBOSE, HBOFE, MTV, MTVH, MTVJ, Cinemax, Showtime.

Pay per view, HDTV, Blu-Ray, digital.

Work more, pay check, pay bills.

Visa, MasterCard, Discover, American Express.

Blackberry, Droid, iTunes, iPhones, iPad, iPod, mp3, Wii, Xbox, Nintendo, Playstation, Fantasy Football.

Internet, Facebook, MySpace, Twitter, YouTube, email, e*trade, ecommerce, text, blog.

Work even more, pay check, and pay even more bills.

Empty, bored, sad, angry, unsatisfied. Just can't put my finger on it.

Have no time for anything. Being idle, being still, being quiet; are you able to do it? Are you able to handle the power going out for one hour? How many times will you flip the light switch? How about the television? Hold on; forget about the power going out and just your computer not moving fast enough? Tapping your pencil; your fingers. "Come on! Come on! Dumb computer." Oh, not you? Never! Yeah, me neither. We live in a world that we have been inundated, bombarded with stimulants; over stimulated. We weren't meant to have so much over load in our minds. It clutters our soul and leads to stress. We need peace.

> "The Lord is my shepherd;
> I shall not want.
> He makes me lie down in green pastures;
> He leads me beside the still waters.
> He restores my soul." – Psalm 23:1-3a

Believing and trusting that God provides all your needs (Philippians 4:19) comes from having an intimate relationship with Him that comes from prayer time and reading His Word. It will grow your trust and faith that all you need for each season of life, of each situation, He imparts. It takes the burden off of you and puts it on the Lord. And this is what He wants. (Matthew 11:28-30)

He restores your soul. God knows that all this is not good for you. He knows what you truly need. The world throws tons of noise. God replenishes us with peace; His peace. Read that preceding scripture. Get a visual of God availing you to receive his peace. Green pastures, still waters; replenishment, restoration, invigoration, enrich. Read it again. He wants you to get away into the countryside, away from the city; the noise, the hassle, and spend time with Him. We look in all the wrong places to find fulfillment. God blesses us with wisdom to wade through the unnecessary temptations to find what is real, true and pure to enrich our lives. Rich pastures and cool streams. I feel that God waits ever so patiently while I putter. We need to make it a habit to be still and not feel we have to check our phone for Facebook, email, texts, etc. You never know when something so important will pop up; can't miss it. What I have found, that helps me, is to take the Bible with me wherever I go. For instance the barber shop; instead of reading People magazine or surfing the internet on my phone, I can lie down in green pastures, sit beside still waters; allowing God to enrich my soul, my spirit.

We will have to deliberately be disciplined to cut out all the surround sound and must clearly define what is important. We must not allow the perpetual noise to lead us to and fro to this and that which only diminishes our efficiency in serving and contributing in the purposes that God desires for each of us. I have been told by some that they can't be disciplined. Again, this allowing worldliness within dictate that you are who you are not. The truth is that God has given you a spirit of discipline. (2 Timothy 1:7). Some things to do can be very hard; but all things are possible with God.

One way, that I have found, that can reduce wasted time is to go to the internet site you needed to go to and then get right off. Surfing the web is not only wasted time but can lead us to sites that are not healthy for us to be exposed to. The same can be said for surfing the tube. And both waste time and lend to a lifestyle less and less full of substance.

Each one of us is like the boy who is exposed to God's will and desire to play the guitar. We are gifted by our creator to use those gifts and talents to bless others; to be an investment in someone else's life. In that story the boy was only distracted by his friends outside playing. How much more pulls us away from that which sharpens us? Be honest with yourself; how often do you intend to do something that is worthwhile but thought to yourself that you were going to, just for a minute, check out Facebook? Our stroll thru the channels and just "see" what's on? I have done just that writing this book. And what happens? An hour or two, a night, a day; wasted. What happens is we get into that habit and that time adds up to a pile of a whole lot of wasted time. And all these things that have become a distraction become necessities. We get dulled. We cannot go 10 minutes without an update. So much so we have a loud beep to alert us of the newest news. We have "real time" news. (Compared to fake time) It's hard to believe that newspapers actually sell. Everything on them happened yesterday. That is so "yesterday." So old. Need it now. We've got to have it now. That is how we are conditioned. Just watch any sports or news channels. There is a continual scroll at the bottom of the screen that has every possible piece of info about anything or everything. It's absurd, but I know I wouldn't have the patience to watch an NFL football game and have to wait until halftime to find out the other scores like I had to when I was a kid. Shoot! Even the 10 minute ticker they came out with in the 90's is too slow.

And in all of this we are becoming like pudding. Pudding sure tastes good. But it doesn't fill you up. It will not give you energy. It doesn't have any lasting value to it. It just tastes good for a second. No meat and potatoes about it. And the substance, the meat and potatoes, is what we are supposed to be about. They are what help us grow up to be big and strong. We only eat pudding after we eat our main food that completes us. We have to be able to discipline ourselves to put aside those non value time wasting short life pleasures and discipline ourselves to seek and do those things that are filling; that which has value, has substance.

We have become pudding eaters with a side of meat and potatoes. Filling up on desserts only leads to cavities and makes us mush. That is what the three ring circus is; a dessert buffet. It looks great, tastes great, not much value. We must get back to placing "value" as a priority. Living a life of excellence is one that we have to discipline ourselves to saying no; to avoiding and ignoring distractions and "stuff" that only clogs and wastes our time.

In Paul's first letter to Timothy, Paul exhorts Timothy not to get caught up in distractions; in pudding. "Exercise yourself toward godliness" – 1 Timothy 4:7b

> "As His divine power has given to us all things that pertain to life and godliness, through the knowledge of Him who called us by glory and virtue." – 2 Peter 1:3

When we get down to it, God has predestined us to live an abundant life that we can actualize with deliberate consistent discipline. If we focus and believe what God says about us; that we must discipline ourselves and that He has equipped us to be disciplined, we can achieve His will for us. It takes work. It takes knowing that you have it in you. It is so important to know that God wills it for you and the enemy tries to divert your focus to pudding.

In the beginning of this chapter I gave you a little piece of a rap from Toby Mac. Two points I want to make. First, the scripture that the song "Lose my soul" comes from Matthew 16:26 "For what profit is it to a man if he gains the whole world, and loses his own soul?" That exhausted list of different time consuming electronics do have some that have become necessities in the world we live in, however the majority of them are just distractions that have consumed us. They consume us trying to get as much stuff as we can get. Pollution. This is the pudding. This is what the enemy would have you be distracted by instead of disciplining yourself to do those things that are life giving, life empowering, life contributing. All that stuff is sound and fury signifying nothing. It is like a three ring circus and our very soul is what is being cheated. Our soul that prospers on seeking to do God's will and purpose. It is our soul that prospers when we do those things that are hard that have sustenance.

The second is what Kirk Franklin, a talented performer in his own right, says right before Toby's little rap.

> Not going to let these material things get in
> my way, man
> I'm trying to get somewhere
> Trying to get somewhere that is real, pure,
> that is true and eternal

Have you ever found yourself realizing that all the "things" you have; all the things that you got because you knew they would make your life better; didn't? That your life wasn't any richer?

Jesus talks to the woman at the well who had five husbands and now was living with another man. Jesus saw that this woman was looking for fulfillment in a husband. She would discard one after she wasn't satisfied and thought she saw exactly what she needed in the next. Husbands could be substituted with many other things; cars, jewelry, clothes, alcohol, gambling, sports, drugs, entertainment, etc. Jesus spoke to this woman where she was trying to unsuccessfully quench her thirst. We all have allowed material things of this world to fool us into thinking they are "just what we need". We chase the brass ring to find out we really are grabbing the empty hole in the middle. What is real, pure, true and eternal is Christ Himself. And that is what He is telling the woman at the well. He tells her eternal truth that all the things of this world fail. He is the eternal fulfillment that our hearts long for. Jesus tells her that He is Living Water.

Jesus answered and said to her," Whoever drinks of this water will thirst again, but whoever drinks of the water that I shall give him will never thirst. But the water that I shall give him will become in him from a fountain of water springing up into everlasting life."

The woman said to Him," Sir, give me this water, that I may not thirst." – John 4:13-15

The woman shows her desperate need to thirst no more and asks to receive the one thing that will fulfill the emptiness she has had all this time. She found truth. She found what is truly real.

Think about that for yourself. Truly, what is real? What do you have in your life that is pure? That which is pure is real. It's not style over substance. It is truly of substance. It is of sustenance to you. Feeds you, grows you, and blesses you. Think of all the stuff that is in your life that isn't real; just has appearance of. These are the things we have that should only be used when we actually need them. For instance; television. Television is great in many ways. Even the entertainment can be when taken in small doses. However we can get so wrapped up in make believe shows that they corrupt our minds and even influence our behavior. They aren't pure. They aren't an ingredient to what is true. But you might say," I need escape." But really it is our soul that craves our creator. We were made to have communion with He that has made us. That is what is real, pure, true and eternal; spending significant time with God. The infilling of His Spirit is what satisfies with His peace, wisdom and discernment.

We all need time to be still. We need this physically, mentally and spiritually. We need to put aside all the sights and sounds of life's circus and regain focus on what are truly priorities in our lives. We need to ask God to open our eyes to that which is in our lives that are not His will for us. When I have sought God in my quiet time of prayer, God will give me a different perspective of things in my life. Where I have convinced myself of something I need to be doing or have to have, God will give me the discernment of how it may be adversely affecting me in accomplishing His purpose in my life. God has shown me in different seasons of my life that there are some time consuming activities that He isn't willing for me to do. It takes discipline to avoid and ignore so much of life's circus but God enables us to do so. It takes seeking Him continually. God wants a personal relationship with you. He desires for you to dwell in His Word. To rest in Him. He wants you to give Him your time and listen to what He puts in your heart. He wants you to heal. He wants you to replenish. God desires that we grasp what is true and real. He wants to give us wisdom to take what we need and lay aside what we don't. In this we can make real the excellence that He will's us to live in.

Maya Moore, All American star, of the record breaking University of Connecticut women's basketball team, was asked how to stay on target to win back to back NCAA Championship's with all the hoopla around their team. Her answer," You just have to discipline yourself to stay focused. You may have to limit your contact with a lot of outside hoopla going on. But I really

think that because it's such a habit for us, it's not hard."
– Associated Press

Discipline is successful when it becomes a habit. We must deliberately focus on what is the most essential in our lives; the real, pure and true.

What are the distractions, material things in your life; keeping you from that which is real, and true, pure and eternal? Sometimes it takes a tragedy or near death experience for us to truly see what is important and what isn't. However, if we seek Him now and that which He offers, we can have it now. We can put aside that which keeps us from what is real, pure, true and eternal. We, therefore, can live a life of excellence.

CHAPTER 3

GOT WILSON?

One of the most popular sitcoms in recent years was *Home Improvement* starring Tim Allen. It was Tim who made the show so popular. Everyone loved Tim. He was so funny and witty and he had a great sidekick in Al. We got much laughs at Al's expense. Tim was always the life of the party. And like most comedies it would usually end with a laugh. However, during a lot of the episodes Tim would have to deal with some tough life situations. There are some circumstances that Tim knew, or quickly found out, that he wasn't going to be able to solve with a quick joke. Sometimes Tim realized that he, like all of us, would find himself in a predicament that he was not able to overcome with his own resources. These situations could have long lasting consequences depending on which way he would go. He would find himself not knowing what to do. Like each of us, he would come to a wall where he would ask himself what in the world to do?

Being so funny and friendly Tim had a lot of friends. He had so many people that would put everything to the side to help out. Tim was a very popular and well liked guy. He had many people he could go to for advice. Al was more than happy to give Tim unsolicited advice on many an occasion. Tim and Al did a lot of things together. Tim did hang out a lot with many people especially his family. But, when Tim needed advice, where did he go? Where he went; was out his back door to the fence that separated his yard from his neighbor's. His neighbor was known as just "Wilson." Actually his name was Wilson Wilson Jr. Yeah; pretty strange. Wilson was in 173 of a possible 203 episodes. More than 80% of all the episodes produced. As much fun as Tim was always having it shows that there were more times, than not advice needed. Why didn't Tim go to Al or one of his other buddies when he needed someone to seriously talk to? Isn't it interesting that when Tim had the real issues of life he went to someone who wasn't his buddy or friend?

Wilson, who was never seen from his chin down, was always behind the fence on his side of the yard and Tim just over the other side. I think that there is strong symbolism with that fence. On Tim's side of the fence were all the people that knew him so well and were definitely bias depending on who they were in Tim's life. Think about the people in your life that you share so much of every day with; spouses, children, parents, siblings, best friends, coworkers. They are the ones that each has their own take on you. Not that this is bad. It is only that a lot of times we cannot be objective because of our close relationship with them. To me that fence represents a line that cannot be crossed with someone who cannot be objective. Someone who doesn't worry about hurting your feelings or telling you just what they see. We don't want to end up being uncomfortable around them and worry that they may be mad at us. Wilson has no emotion or history with Tim tied into their relationship. If Tim would get mad at Wilson because he didn't like what Wilson said Wilson wouldn't lose any sleep. Wilson doesn't have anything to lose by offending Tim with the truth. He isn't worried that Tim will not invite him over to the next social gathering at Tim's. He had never been invited. He wouldn't worry about a mutual friend being upset with him. They didn't share the same friends. Wilson is exactly what Tim needed. Wilson is the one we all need. We all need a Wilson in our life. When Tim would go over to speak with Wilson he knew that Wilson would hear him out. Tim knew that whatever he asked Wilson he would get straight truth. Wilson would listen and he would answer only what he would know. His cool demeanor gave Tim peace. He knew he could count on Wilson. Wilson would always bring to light to Tim something that Tim was missing. At times Tim couldn't see because he was too involved in it. Tim always felt that Wilson would give him his true advice, assessment, observation, regardless of how Tim would respond. Tim would frequent the fence more and more because he found someone who would direct him without trying to take over the wheel.

There was a young boy who was walking in the woods and he saw a man chopping a tree down with an ax. The man was throwing all his might behind the ax that swung violently into the tree. Each time the man did it big chunks of wood would go flying off of it and in a few minutes the tree would come slamming down to the ground. He watched the man for a little while and then went home. The little boy would go in the woods and he would see this man every time. He noticed that it was taking longer and longer for the man to chop the tree down. He observed that the man seemed to exert more and more energy getting less and less of the tree at each swing. One day he saw the man with his hands on his knees catching his breath. The man was sweating profusely. The man would finally stand upright, grab his ax, take a deep breath, and take his swing. He didn't make much of a cut into the tree. The man stopped again to regain his strength and energy. As he did this the boy approached him. The man, wiping sweat off his brow, looked up at the boy. "Sir," he asked, "your ax is very dull. Why don't you stop and go get it sharpened?" The man, with a slight smile, responded, "Oh son, I don't have the time to do that, I need to get these tree's cut down."

January 2008. Ax was dull. I didn't have the time to sharpen it. I was preparing for and leading three Biblical meetings, teaching adult Sunday school and working in ministry for the Fellowship of Christian Athletes. I was very busy. I had a lot of people depending on me. And I was as dry as a desert and had no idea that I was thirsting. The last week of that month I was invited to come to a Christian mentoring school named Mentoring Men for the Master. It was held at a church on the other side of town. It was at 6am on Saturday. I walked into a room that had about 50 men. These 50 men were praying and sharing. I was introduced to Dr. Bill Bennett. He spoke on being obedient to God's word and to doing what the word of God commanded whether you felt like it or not. He would speak scriptures that commanded man on different things. I was convicted. I was doing parts of the bible that I felt like doing. I wasn't being challenged to do anymore than that. I thought pretty good of myself as a Christian. I didn't have anyone holding me accountable. I had no idea that my ax was dull because I had no reason to examine it. I wasn't being graded. I didn't have anyone looking over my shoulder making sure that I was advancing in my walk with God. If you don't have someone pushing you, do you have the discipline to do it yourself? It wasn't until this Saturday morning did I realize that I needed fresh water. I was dry and now I realized it because I was exposed to it. I needed a mentor.

Dr. Bennett was led by God to leave the pulpit of a thriving church of 8,000 and begin to disciple men; a few at a time. For the last few years he has been pouring out his life coming along side men challenging and encouraging them to be accountable to obedience to God's will and commands. He spoke to me after class and asked me some very challenging questions about my accountability to doing what the scriptures called a man to do and be. Accountable? I was like most men, I guess. There were things I did and things I didn't.

Within the next few weeks he asked to meet with me. He asked questions about my prayer life, Bible reading and meditation. He asked me many questions about the Bible to which I didn't have the answers. He would challenge me to read books and he would test me on the chapters. I couldn't half way do it for the results would show. What did it do for me? It grew me. It made me stretch out of my comfort zone and apply myself in ways I haven't before. It has grown me as a husband and father. My relationship with my wife grows more and more toward the model of marriage that God has ordained. Also, I have become more of a father to my children in line with Biblical teaching. Becoming more accountable to God has enabled me to hold other men accountable.

What I have realized over the last few years being mentored by Dr. Bennett is that he knew I was dry before I did. How did he know? Because I drove half an hour to be at a mentoring school at 6am on a Saturday. To get up that early there has got to be something within that isn't satisfied; a craving, a hunger, a yearning. It wasn't until I humbled myself to this truth and acknowledge the need that I began to get replenished.

What have I learned over these last few years? I have learned that most men are too unwilling, too prideful, too comfortable, too undisciplined, to be challenged to do what they don't want to do but need to do. Jesus spent 3 years pouring His life into 12 men. He challenged them, encouraged them and humbled them when pride got in the way. Dr. Bennett has done the same with me and many men. He has helped many men internalize and meditate on the word of God in order to conform into the image of Christ. Jesus taught them how to live their lives according to God's way instead of man's way. You don't find too many men who are willing to do that.

The man in the woods was too blinded in what he thought he had to do to see the truth in what the boy was saying to him. We all need to listen to what someone else might have to say. We do not know it all. The funny thing is that no one ever says they know it all but at times contrast. We do this by never listening and acting on someone's advice.

My question for you is; do you have a mentor? Do you have someone who is more mature than you that can give you insight that you would actually act upon? Do you have someone who you meet with a couple of times a month that you can glean from? Someone who isn't afraid to tell you like it is and how you can change it? Dr. Bennett had no problem telling me that he loved me and that because of that he would tell me some things that I needed to work on in order to become a more effective leader and teacher. Sometimes I would say "ouch, that hurt." He did it, though, because I needed to hear it. We can all be so immersed and busy that we can't see where we need improvement.

Are you able to be honest and say that there are places in your life that need improvement and change and do not know what they are? I was and didn't even know it. See, by that time in January 2008 I would be in prayer a lot early in the morning crying out to God for help. I wasn't preparing well for the ministries I was responsible for. I didn't see much coming from them. I was frustrated. I felt heavily burdened. I questioned whether I should be in these positions of leadership and teaching. I opened up to God and He opened me up to being a student.

The week before I went to Mentoring Men for the Master I facilitated a monthly Saturday morning breakfast for men to come and fellowship and I would get someone to talk to the men. On this particular Saturday I had asked Billy Williams, who I had met through a Fellowship of Christian Athletes function, if he would come speak at this breakfast. Did he ever; with such vigor and enthusiasm with a very definite focus. He spoke how just a few years earlier he was smoking crack and drinking a fifth of whiskey a day. His life was a mess. His mother would try and get him to go to church. He would start going, sometimes drunk, sometimes high.

He would sit in the back sobbing knowing he needed a change or his life was over. He would go to church and listen to the sermon but it wasn't changing him. Dr. Bennett was asked to speak to him by Billy's mother. He went to Billy who was sitting in the back of the church one Sunday. He asked Billy if Billy wanted to live. Billy said he did. Dr. Bennett then committed to mentoring Billy; coming along side him encouraging him, loving him, but also he held Billy accountable. Making Billy get up early every morning and being in prayer. He gave Billy scripture to memorize and then to meditate on the scripture and pray on it. Dr. Bennett would have Billy meet with him to pray and to teach him. Dr. Bennett held Billy accountable to know the scriptures, to read and take notes on books Dr. Bennett required Billy to read. Billy's life has been transformed because his life was now based on the truth; the Living Word of God.

It is when someone cares enough about you that they will pour their life into you. That is what is needed in this culture, this society, we live in. We need others who can help us to get all of our potential out of us by holding us accountable to doing so.

> "Getting men to do the things they don't want to do in order to achieve the things they want." – Tom Landry, former football coach, Dallas Cowboys, 5 Superbowl appearances

In order to love a life of excellence we have to be lead. We have to be coachable; teachable. We have to be honest . Are you teachable? Will you be humble enough that you will allow constructive criticism be given to you? Will you allow someone into your life that will lead you to excellence even though it will cost you your pride and ego? Will you be challenged to be held accountable? It took me going to Mentoring Men for the Master to realize and confess that I needed direction; that I needed a mentor.

In *Live the Life Abundant* I tell of being challenged by my friend and college roommate Pat Harmon. Pat convinced me that if I would listen and work with him that he would help me be prepared when the opportunity would come to start at receiver for our college football team. The indelible moment that I spoke of is when we went running up a winding ascending street after working out on a field in the middle of a hot summer day. Looking back I realize that Pat was not only mentoring me but was being held accountable himself. When we first started running we were side by side. Pat was encouraging me the whole time as he was also running. He didn't drive to the top of the hill and yell down to me to start running and that he would time me. No, he ran besides me challenging me and encouraging me. After a while he ran up to the top of the hill. There he slid into the mentor role. He was prodding me on to do something that he was willing to do; and did do. When I wanted to stop he urged me to continue to battle that I could, just as he did, make it to the top. Pat wouldn't let me quit. How many of us have that? How many of us have someone that just tells us to not worry about it and quit and let's go eat ice cream. Actually, we do need people to chill and eat ice cream with. But more importantly we need someone who will not allow us to settle for less than we are. I will tell you that, absolutely , I would not be authoring books, speaking before audiences and leading and teaching if I didn't persevere and get up to the top of the hill. I believe, without a doubt, the confidence that I gained that year, becoming a starter, gave me the confidence and courage to do that which I am doing; sowing excellence into the life of others. If Pat didn't hold me to that standard of excellence it would have never came to fruition.

> "And the things that you have heard from me among many witnesses, commit these to faithful men who will be able to teach others also." – 2 Timothy 2:2

Living a life of excellence is a sowing and reaping process that we are all connected. If you do not seek to become the excellence in you how many people will be affected? If married, your spouse? Children? Co-worker, friends? The people they all come in contact with? To live a life of excellence you have to first be exposed to it. If everyone decided to be selfish who would ever become selfless? If Pat didn't care enough to help me I wouldn't be in the position to be capable of helping others. If Dr. Bennett was self centered and selfish and wasn't obedient to God to make a radical change in his life and begin to mentor men in small groups, one on one, I wouldn't of been challenged in my spiritual walk. I wouldn't be able to be used by God as much because I wouldn't be disciplined as much, obedient as much, as I have become. We are extremely blessed and gifted. We have a great responsibility to be a conduit for those blessing and gifts for others.

> "For everyone to whom much is given, from him much will be required; and to whom much has been committed, of him they will ask the more." – Luke 12:48b

The ripple effect of lives touched by Dr. Bennett is astonishing. The testimonies, not only from lay persons, but also pastors and others in ministry, stretch long. Even if the only life that was affected by Dr. Bennett's obedience was that of Billy Williams, it would be more than enough. For Billy is sowing into the lives of countless people. The impact is endless. So, though, is the impact of not living out the life God has intended for you. Each one is different, but in the end it is to bring a light of excellence for others to begin to yearn for themselves.

> "So, affectionately longing for you, we were
> well pleased to impart to you not only
> the gospel of God, but also our own lives,
> because you had become dear to us."
> – 1 Thessalonians 2:8

The effective profound affect that you can have on someone is when they see how much you love them. When you care so much for someone, as Dr. Bennett does for me and so many others, you pour out all that you have been blessed with to share it with them also. Living a life of excellence is giving out your life that others may prosper.

In order to live a life of excellence you must come to a place where you realize you aren't living that life. Be real with yourself and ponder those questions that I ask in this chapter.

I believe that every day you are to be taught. Every day you are to teach.

I believe that every day you are to listen. Every day you are to speak.

I believe that every day you are to sow. Every day you are to reap.

I believe that every day you are to be mentored. Every day you are to mentor.

I believe that every day you must be held accountable. Every day you are to hold someone else accountable.

Mentoring Men for the Master has each man have an accountability partner. They would be someone, like yourself, who is striving to be disciplined in living a godly life. In which, of course, in our society, is very difficult. Therefore, we need to stick side by side one another and encourage each other to keep striving forward in excellence while all around us settles in the pool of mediocrity and indifference. We influence one another positively or negatively. We need to find someone who is willing to keep you honest as you keep them honest. We all need an accountability partner. Someone who will help us grow.

> "As iron sharpens iron, so a man sharpens
> the countenance of his friend."
> – Proverbs 27:17

Do you have someone in your life that mentors you? Someone who is more spiritually mature than you that have a strong walk with God? If you do not, pray that God will put a person in your path and that you will have wisdom to recognize that person. Throughout the Bible both men and women had persons that they had in their lives that mentored them. The ultimate mentor is

Jesus. He mentored 12 men for 3 years and changed the whole world. How about you? Will you allow Him to be your ultimate mentor?

That is the everlasting life of excellence.

CHAPTER 4

2 1 1

211? What significance does that number have? It doesn't really have any. Does anything jump to your mind? No, it is probably insignificant. Think about it, do you ever feel insignificant? Have you ever felt that you have lived that saying; sound and fury signifying nothing? Running, but seemingly going nowhere, but backwards? Out of breath, out of money, out of options? I believe everyone in the room raises their hand. At one point or another we have. The sad thing about it is how close we are to 212. How unaware we are of how close and we give up.

> "And let us not grow weary while doing good, for in due season we shall reap if we do not lose heart." – Galatians 6:9

At times it doesn't feel like our heart is in it. We get so motivated to start an endeavor. We might feel inspired and energetic. We feel a calling, a challenge, an aspiration. We have a visual of how it will turn out; achievement, accomplishment, a finished work. Victory! We put in the discipline, the sacrifice, the hard work. We might have setbacks, negative responses or just no visual progress. We push on, focus, concentrate, work even harder and still might not see evidence of development. We can become discouraged and feel disillusioned by it all. We start allowing distractions and false beliefs to come into our minds. I know that I have had thoughts of," what was I thinking? Crazy to think I could do this. Such and such was right, I can't do this; it's a pipe dream." We not only can become discouraged, but might start thinking negatively about ourselves. That is why it is so important to be encouraged by the Living Word. One of the reasons that I had pushed through in writing books, trudging through with a business during the recession and other undertakings is scriptures such as the aforementioned Galatians 6:9. I believe it is so important to know and meditate on the word of God in order to get by feelings and emotions and what others might negatively say. So many times we get stuck on 211; worn out. Is it worth it? To give up when we are there and not realize we are that close. That close to 212.

212? Does that number have any significance? It has incredible implications in our life right now. 212 degrees Fahrenheit. At 211 degrees Fahrenheit you have extremely hot water that can scold you. At 212 degrees Fahrenheit you have boiling water that can kill germs as well as produce steam that can power a locomotive. Just 1 degree. But what a huge and life changing degree it is. It is the huge difference of hot water to powerful steam. God has willed each of us to have a 212 degree in our lives that He wants and desires for us. He also has given us examples of those who have gone before us that we can gain encouragement and motivation to stick with it. We have persons before us that challenge us to strive even farther. I would like to see an athlete, who achieves so much on the playing field that the team is going to retire his number, decline. Instead of retiring his number he wants to challenge someone to wear it and have even more success than he did. That is living the life of excellence that others can visualize more success because they first saw you. You can be that great example.

Think of all the sports records that have stood the test of time. There are some records that many believe can never be broken.

Wilt Chamberlain scoring 100 points in one game, 1962, 55 rebounds in one game, 1960.

Joe DiMaggio's 56 game hitting streak, 1941.
Ted Williams hitting .400 for the Sox in 1941.

Cal Ripken playing in 2,632 consecutive baseball games over a span of almost 2 decades (80's, 90's).

Georgia Tech beating Cumberland College by 222 in football, 220-0, in 1916.

Oklahoma University football not losing in 47 consecutive football games, 1953-1957.

UCLA basketball winning 7 National titles in a row, 1967-73.

North Carolina Women's soccer – 103 consecutive games without a loss, 1986-90.

I am sure there are others that will last forever in the opinions of many. Many of these records are believed to never be accomplished again. However, there was one sport statistic that was seen as humanly impossible; the four minute mile.

Whenever a ceiling is placed, limitations set; they are for the most part accepted. If they are accepted than they aren't challenged, usually. In 1954, at the Iffley Road Track in Oxford, England, Roger Bannister challenged a paradigm in the road racing world. He set out to prove that a sub 4 minute mile was possible. It is a time that hadn't been tried or accomplished, ever. For us to lead a life of excellence we must use every resource we have available to us, especially our mind. That is what Roger Bannister did. He knew that he would need motivation during the run as well as when he was preparing. He enlisted a couple of running friends who would run hard for small stretches allowing another to take over when he couldn't keep up the pace. This way they were running at a faster clip than they could if they were running for a whole mile. This strategy gave Bannister such a test to keep pace that someone who was running the race for the entire mile couldn't do. On May 6, 1954 British med student Roger Bannister ran the mile in 3 minutes, 59.4 seconds. At this time there had been nearly 100 years of accurate recorded 1 mile runs. And not one recorded 4 minute mile. In the 50 years since then almost 1,000 runners have broken that mark in official sanctioned races. The first American was in 1957. American Jim Ryun became the first high school runner to do it, in 1964, as a junior. American Steve Scott has recorded over 100 mile runs under the 4 minute mark.

Why had no one run the sub 4 minute mile, and then when Roger Bannister did, so many others also were able? It was no longer impossible. It had been accomplished. "If he could do it why can't I?" Began to prevail. Someone had done it so there was a ceiling that could be broken through. All of these sub 4 runners were able to prepare and visualize breaking the mark because it had been done. Someone else went to the extreme, and did so, that others could be even more excellent.

Social learning theory is when you model the behavior you observe in someone else. We live in a culture that has taken this theory and branded it. Instead of being inspired to greatness we have too many examples mediocrity being more than accepted, rewarded. Instead of students working hard to achieve valedictorian in their schools officials believe that it's unfair to the others who do really good but aren't the very best. So they are going to have more than one valedictorian, which contradicts the definition. There are places where they don't want children to have grades because it will hurt their esteem. We are socially learning mediocrity that is decreasing incentive for striving toward excellence. We therefore must be agents for excellence. We each, individually, have a responsibility to interrupt this lethargy to ingenuity. We must go against the stream. We must take the harder road. We must seek to see the trap and move away from it.

> "And do not be conformed to this world, but be transformed by the renewing of your mind." – Romans 12:2a

Romans 12:1-2; from Eugene Peterson's *The Message*:

> "So here's what I want you to do, God helping you. Take your everyday, ordinary life-your sleeping, eating, going-to-work,

and walking-around life-and place it before God as an offering. Embracing what God does for you is the best thing you can do for him. Don't become so well- adjusted to your culture that you fit into it without even thinking. Instead fix your attention on God. You'll be changed from the inside out. Readily recognize what he wants from you, and quickly respond to it. Unlike the culture around you, always dragging you down to its level of immaturity. God brings the best out of you, develops well-formed maturity in you.

"Don't become so well-adjusted to your culture." We certainly can without knowing it. We are like that frog who is put into lukewarm water. The temp satisfies him and he becomes comfortable. He becomes unaware of the rising temperature because it is being done very subtly. Before too long the frog is boiled. If the frog was put into the water when it was already boiling it would jump out. It would be such a shock of pain it wouldn't give the water any chance to cook him. We see every day the effects of subtle acceptance of behaviors and attitudes that were once seen as improper. We must set for ourselves standards that are higher than the ever increasing lowered standards of our culture. We must be conscientious that being in our culture we might naturally bend toward that immaturity. It is a lot easier to go with the flow. It is like someone who moves to another part of the country and everyone there notices his accent and theirs to him. However after some time that person's accent becomes more and more like the people he is now surrounded with. That is our natural tendencies. That is why we have to be aware and deliberate in seeking to become all that God had intended for you. Though our culture has become acceptable to what God says is immoral, sinful, we are to take higher ground. This is what our children need to see. This is what the world around us needs to see. We must be forever mindful that God's standards are much higher than the standards set by the culture that we live in. We need to surround ourselves with others who believe the same. Iron sharpens iron.

> "Let your light so shine before men, that they may see your good works and glorify your Father in heaven." – Matthew 5:16

The first thing is that we need to strive forward from doing what we want to doing what we should. In the preceding chapter, Got Wilson, I talk about how I had other men that God has used to hold me accountable. Not only accountable, but as examples of men seeking to live in obedience to God. These men, who showed me Christ like examples, have come along side me encouraging me to do the same. It is totally different than all I see around me; and harder. That is why we need encouragers; pacesetters.

That is the second thing. We need encouragement. We need to see others who do the hard thing even when they have themselves been discouraged.

What are some desires of your heart you have shelved due to being discouraged? We always consider why we can't do something. We come up with dozens of reasons why not. I spoke in *Live the Life Abundant* of how you are told no, can't, don't some 20,000 times by the time you are 18 years old. We are programmed to jump ship the first sign of adversity. The day Roger Bannister ran that first recorded sub 4 minute mile there were crosswinds up to 25 miles an hour. This meant that no matter what direction he was facing while running the wind was going to be hitting him on the side of his body which would make it difficult to run optimal time. He could have easily reasoned that it would be impossible to do the impossible on this day because of the conditions. Listen when I tell you- The conditions will never be right! Not all of them. If it wasn't the crosswinds it would be the temperature. If not the temperature it would be raining out. Maybe kids chucking rocks at him! Knights in armor attacking him! Lions and tigers and bears, oh my! Foolish? We turn mole hills into mountains. Well of course, then, we can't do it. Seems silly. But that is what we do when we get one little inkling that we might not succeed. We then put it off for another day; a day when all the stars align just right. Good intentions are just that, good intentions.

Zig Ziglar speaks about this in one of his books about good intentions going nowhere. A certain person is determined to _____ (you fill in the blank for yourself) But am not able to do it during Thanksgiving holiday. There is so much to get ready for, family coming in town. Thanksgiving weekend comes and goes. Oh my goodness December 1st! Christmas is in 3 ½ weeks! There is so much shopping to do. Kids Christmas plays; decorations to put up, inside and outside the house. 3 ½ weeks fly by. Christmas is over. But this person will wait until after New Years Day. Start fresh, like a New Years resolution. The holiday blues. Get started next month. But is February, cold and snowy. The person decides to wait until spring comes. Spring births optimism and energy and motivation. However March brings the kids baseball and softball seasons. Kids have practices and games. Driving here and there, season will be over and then be able to do _____. Season is over, school is out and summer is here; vacations, beach, summer camp for the kids. How many times do we say that summer went by so fast? But with the kids back in school it will be ideal time for _____. However, we will have to wait until after the first couple of weeks of school. There is so much the kids have to get going with in their classes. We need to let them settle in. School projects, football games and Halloween! Thanksgiving is in a couple of weeks. After Thanksgiving is over it will be the ideal time for _____; perfect conditions for _____.

The truth is…life is short. And your life is of incredible value. God has put desires in your heart of those things for you to accomplish, to experience. There are those things in life that we must deliberately keep our focus on and, at times, trudge through, in order to experience that overwhelming feeling of completion, success, triumph.

Many a person where stuck on 211 and had every reason to quit and not ever see their desires attained. One that comes to mind is Walt Disney. Here is the thing. What if he gave up when the going was tough and it looked like he would never see his vision of that incredible theme park come to reality? He had a desire and a vision that no one, at that time, thought was realistic. Now try to imagine what never got imagined. The incredible creativity is that which spurred the theme parks and movies which have given others the foundation to build on. Roger Bannister gave many a credible reality of what can be done as far as time in the mile run. The impetus that Walt Disney gave to the world of entertainment and the arts is farther reaching than we could ever know. Walt Disney striving forward and achieving the impossible fulfilled him, but how much more each of us. The power of the fulfillment of 212 is farther reaching than you; it is a blessing to so many others. What is your 212? Will you seek to do it that others may benefit? That you would be blessed as you bless others?

That is living a life of excellence.

Take time and consider. Honestly, what have been or are your 211? What can you do to attain 212? Are you allowing sin to weigh you down; keep you from actualizing God's 212 for you? Think about it, write it down, and pray on it. If God gave you the desire, He has given you the resources.

Be a source for someone else to aspire to live in excellence.

CHAPTER 5

ARTIFICIALLY FLAVORED

It has been more than a few years, but I remember clearly as I drove up into the Mohawk Valley, upstate New York. It was early in the morning before the sun was to come up. It was rolling hills and beautiful mountain range. It was early spring and Marlies and I were going to her hometown. It was my first time with her to where she grew up on farm lands; riding horses on wide spans of unadulterated countryside. We were not yet engaged to be married but it must have been serious, for even though I had met her parents, it was now to meet both of her grandmothers.

What struck me so much as we drove that early morning was the natural feel. There weren't any commercial signs around interrupting the night except for lights down by the barns on the farms. Marlies told me that the farmers were already up and milking the cows. How simply wholesome that seemed to me. As we made it to her hometown I met a lot of her family; aunts and uncles, cousins, grandparents and family friends. It was Easter and the whole family would come together. Marlies's mom and grandmother would be in the kitchen putting together all kinds of great tasting dishes together. The food was going to be served downstairs. As I walked around the house there were many family pictures. Every room was so warm and inviting. Everything was so simple. It seems such a contrast to so many houses in new "subdivisions" that seem to try to be showy and impressive, cold and untouchable. This house, which Marlies's grandparents have lived in for 50 years, was like a favorite pair of sweats or sweater. It fits perfectly snug and comfy. This was the home Marlies's mom, aunt and uncle grew up in. It had such an authenticity which is less and less valued this day and age. The atmosphere in the house was one of hospitality and genuineness. Marlies grew up the hill from her grandmother's house, right next to her other grandmother's house. Since we had time before we were to eat we went up the street to there. There was a field across the street where there was a horse grazing. Marlies squinted and smiled. After all these years, it was her horse, Zipper, now owned by another family on a farm across the street. We drove to the very top of this mountain that she had lived off of. Wow, you could see the whole valley spread out before you; trees, farms and fields, nothing but green. All natural.

We made our way back to her grandparents house for dinner and we headed down the stairs to the basement where the folded tables were put together for the Thanksgiving feast. After we made our way down stairs she showed me this room called the "fruit cellar". In this room were shelves and shelves of canned fruits and vegetables that her grandparents grew in their garden that they had canned; corn, beans, asparagus, beets, pickles, and jams and jellies; rhubarb, gooseberry, blackberry, strawberry. They also had this huge freezer of all the vegetables they had frozen. Milk crates and crates full of potatoes. All of these homemade foods to last for a long time; pure and natural.

Up the road where Marlies's other grandparents had lived they had real maple syrup. Marlies's father and grandfather would stick spouts into maple trees that the sap would run into buckets that were hanging from the spouts. They would set these up at the beginning of winter. All winter long they would pour the maple sap into a big black cauldron that was continually over flames. There was always someone making sure the fire was going. The heating and stirring would process the sap into syrup. The syrup was canned/ bottled. It was two steps from the tree to the cauldron to the can/jar; real, pure, natural. It tasted…ow, gosh it was awful! This certainly was not Aunt Jemima, no Log Cabin. How could anyone stomach this? I could live without cable TV if absolutely had to. (Did for the first 10 years of my life). I have survived without computers, cell phones and DVD players. What else? Well I am sure I can think of other things. But I love pancakes and I need the REAL thing on them. That is what I consider the real thing which is what I have been programmed by taste buds to believe is the real thing. That of course is the fake thing; the artificially flavored maple syrup without the maple. As I sit here writing, I pull out our syrup bottle from the pantry, and look on the back label. No natural about it. Probably more than just those two steps used to make the real syrup in the Mohawk Valley and not a Maple tree around. There is one ingredient that I wouldn't dare try to pronounce and has 17 letters in it. Boy! Is there a lot of sugar in this! And I will tell you what. It is good. I love it. I pour on a lot of it on my pancakes, French toast. For me; nothing like the real stuff. I don't like the pure, natural real Maple syrup; the Maple that comes from a Maple tree. The syrup that doesn't have all the artificial fillers to make it taste good, but aren't good for me. This is one example of style over substance. This is one example of me being artificially flavored; just one example of being drawn away from truth to convenience. We live in a culture full of it.

It isn't that the real syrup looked any different than the fake syrup. I wouldn't know the difference unless I tasted it. In that case it is very different.

There is the problem. It is epidemic in our world. Coke's slogan is "the real thing." But we have been so removed from the real thing in our lives that the real thing becomes inconvenient, foreign, and too hard. Doesn't taste good!

Go back to the maple syrup. It would take a little while, but I could do it. I could start substituting the fake stuff with the real thing. In my preceding book *Live the Life Abundant* I talk about going from white enriched flour to real wheat in pancakes, bread and pasta and how it took awhile for my taste buds to get used to the taste and that now it is what seems normal. In doing so, not only myself, but my whole family is eating much healthier. And so goes the same with the Maple syrup. It would be natural and good for my body compared to store bought syrup's.

OK. So what am I getting at? We have been duped in our culture today in so many areas of our lives and don't even realize that we are selling ourselves short. What is even worse is that if you talk to most people they are ambivalent about it. Style over substance. If it is easier we do it. It has a lot to do with discipline. Disciplining ourselves to substance, delayed gratification. We are bombarded with the marketing machine through media to have it now, you deserve it, get it. And do it now. We have become robots in that we are being dictated in what, when and how. What is acceptable and what is the new norm. Things 20 years ago that we wouldn't in anyway be swayed because of core beliefs in what is right and good have been blurred that we can be coerced into accepting. I watched in an interview a man who managed mortgages say just that regarding qualifying individuals for mortgage loans. He said that 10, 15 years ago that there was a standard of what was responsible and prudent. It was accepted and right. Over time with personal greed and lax on requirements for loans, different avenues were used to make deals "work." Alternative ways of allowing people to be approved for mortgage loans that they really couldn't afford were being passed through. Why? Money. Companies and individuals were making a lot of money. Now, this guy that was on this program being interviewed said he didn't have a choice but to get on board with this new paradigm. His company, and he, wouldn't survive if they didn't, like the industry, allow loans that years before were seen as irresponsible to allow. For what is real and solid has been replaced with what is convenient and satisfying; artificially flavored. Unfortunately, consequences are felt by everyone. Even those people who live and spend correctly and are fiscally responsible are affected. I believe it is a big reason that our economy is in the shape that it is in now. As well as the spiritual, mental, financial and physical shape of so many people. We buy and eat anything we want when we want it. We get into debt getting what we want when we want. We have been programmed to find our fulfillment in things and we feed our appetites in the same way. There is; however, repercussions. We are free to make our choices but are not free of the consequences. Let me say that again. We are free to make our choices but not free of the consequences. What happens is that we have lost true sense of what is really fulfilling. What was God's original intent to be satisfying to our minds, body and Spirit, are from Him. They come from what He created; what is natural and real. Not something that on its own doesn't stand up unless it is souped up with unnatural things; such as Maple syrup.

What has become the challenge for us is that we have been programmed by our culture to take an easier way, less complicated, quicker way. Not that any are wrong, but some do not hold up. We surrender quality for trendy, appealing and cool. In general, we have lost the discipline to take the time to get things right. That is why the industry of making natural maple syrup is all but extinct. It takes too long and is too costly. It is easier to make something that isn't the real thing and stick a label on it that it is.

Marlies's family would stick those spouts directly into the maple tree and it would take 30 gallons of sap to make 1 gallon of syrup. Sap goes from the roots to the limbs to put leaves on the branches. It would bring the tree back to life every spring. The sun shining would trigger the limbs to begin the process. The spouts would gather the sap as it ran back and forth from the roots and the limbs. This would begin to happen once the temperatures would rise into the 30's. They would have to wait until that time, whenever it would come. It made for ideal circumstances except for the east wind blowing. For whatever reason the tree just didn't produce when the wind came from the east.

They would use a rayon clothe to strain the maple of all impurities. They would use a certain type of barometer that would read the density of the syrup for just the right consistency. Do we use barometers in our own lives to check ourselves? This is where we have to be honest with ourselves. If we continue to take the easy, artificial path can we be able to take the genuine harder one when we don't have a choice? The person that doesn't have air conditioning or cable in his house has a lot less of a time when the power goes out then us who are so conditioned by them. When I was growing up we and so many of our neighbors had big gardens. For the most part we could survive if we had to if money got real tight and groceries became sparse. You see what I am getting at? When we become less self reliant we become precariously dependant on others. I, like everyone, is glad to live with the many conveniences of modern technology and services. But, just as the syrup from the maple tree is filtered and strained to find the right consistency, we must likewise.

We live in a world that celebrates style over substance. We have become so well adjusted to the flare and theatrics we become dulled and snowed over to what is genuine and authentic; those things that hold weight and have lasting value. Style is empty calories. Substance is that which will empower us, strengthen and inspire us.

I know for myself that I have to check myself. We are told in Romans 12:3 to be honest with ourselves in our self evaluation. What are those things that are artificial in my life? What would it take to be more authentic? All you have to do is watch a couple of minutes of most reality shows and you will see empty calories, pudding.

Looks great, tastes great, without any lasting value. And these shows are popular and many aspire to have just as what they see on them. It is the artificial that is so enticing. After the lights and fanfare disappear I wonder how fulfilled those people truly are in their lives. We read about too many athletes and celebrities that have a life of ruin, end up in prison, commit suicide, murdered or die prematurely, just a short time after the fame and money. The artificial flavor sooner or later doesn't hold up.

I believe that if you are honest you can find things in your life that you put so much value into, that really aren't. I know I do. God has really worked on me with how I can waste so much time on such insignificant things. This left less time for the things of value. Things of value usually take time, sacrifice and work. Living a life of excellence is a continuing progression of character building.

I have found that the more I identify and discard the artificial in my life, the more I find time for that which is legitimate. That which is authentic is what builds a solid foundation in being strong, reliable and efficient. In *Live the Life Abundant* I talk about how putting aside hours and hours of television and focusing on reading and prayer enabled me to grow more and more in who I am and the gifts and talents I have been given, and how to use them.

> "Therefore whoever hears these sayings of Mine, and does them, I will liken him to a wise man who built his house on the rock: and the rain descended, the floods came, and the winds blew and beat on that house;

and it did not fall, for it was founded on
the rock.

"But everyone who hears these sayings of
Mine, and does not do them, will be like
a foolish man who built his house on the
sand: and the rain descended, the floods
came, and the winds blew and beat on that
house; and it fell. And great was its fall."
– Matthew 7:26-27

When I read this scripture, and give it thought, one
thing keeps coming to mind. Jesus knew. I, as everyone,
would face many trials and tribulations (John 16:33)
and how we would fare is in what we put our time
and faith in; Him or the world. I write in the chapter,
Three Ring Circus, of all the things we get consumed
with that we end up putting so much time and thought
into. The reality is that those things will do us almost
no good in the hardships of life. The solid foundation
is faith in Him and those teachings that will grow us to
be steady and firm in the storms of life. However, I can
be just like Israel in the Old Testament. When things
are going well I can lose that focus and get caught up of
the appealing things of the world. Then, when trouble
comes, I run back to God pleading for help. The Word
tells us to be continually in Him. Continual obedience
has helped me to stay focused on Him throughout the
very rough financial times that I have dealt with during
this recession. If I didn't have a strong relationship with
God and building my faith through prayer and His word
I would be a complete mess. And that would have a
direct affect on my wife and children, who look to me
for assurance during times like this. Keeping my focus on

Him has allowed my family's focus on me to be one that they can rely on.

In chapter 14 of the book of Matthew we read of Jesus walking on the water toward the frightened disciples. They are holding on as the wind and waves toss the boat around. As a lot of our situations, they didn't have control. Jesus spoke to them and told them to be of courage for He was amongst them. Peter asked Him to allow himself to walk on water if it was indeed Him (Him being, not only Jesus, but God). Jesus told him to come forward; and he did. Peter walked on water as he kept his eyes on Jesus. But as soon as he took his eyes off Jesus, and put his focus on the wind and waves, he began to sink. Jesus reached down and pulled him up. If we continue to focus on Jesus and His teachings we are able to grow in that which is of value; the teachings of Jesus. He gives us these teachings for He knows it is what we will need as a solid foundation for anything of value that we put interest into. Regardless of wherever you put your talents and gifts into; that career, activities, interests, services, family, marriage, others; build on the solid foundation that is Jesus Christ. So, for when the storms come; and they will come, you will be at the best to withstand them.

It is about discipline. It isn't about avoiding and ignoring all that is frivolous. It is, though, putting them in their place. Decades ago, those things were just a minor, small distraction from that which we needed to do. Now we have individuals who suffer from the ailment known as joystick thumb. Heard that one? It is a kind of carpal tunnel syndrome on the thumb from overuse of a joystick from a video game. We have lively debates about reality television shows. More people have enough knowledge for that debate than on the issues that have a real affect on our lives. We have become undisciplined. We have persons that spend hours a day on Facebook. It becomes a lifestyle. A lifestyle with the minimum required of substance; full of style, little to no value. It takes discipline to say enough is enough and engage in real life. Knowing what is going on around you and how they affect you. We become apathetic to real issues that are in our world. We have, comparatively to the past, had low voter turnout nationally and locally in elections. People are less and less informed. Not because it is being withheld, but because so many people don't care enough to put down the fun stuff and pay attention to what is going on around them; me included. Then, people get furious when they find out a new law or tax. "No one asked me!" Yes, they actually did; it's called voting.

When I made the choice, some ten years ago, to turn off the television (*Live the Life Abundant*, page 9), and got back to reading and prayer, it began a process of being disciplined to put down flippant stuff and focus on the important things of life. I was, like many people, building my foundation on sand. Those things won't hold me up when I need to delve into resources that have been built up within. I was spending hours upon hours watching television and playing sports.

I had found that once I began to discipline myself I became more conscious of the going on around me. (Still a work in progress) I also became sensitive to my gifts and talents and sought how to apply them to serving others. When I became more disciplined I became less selfish and more servant centered.

How does this tie into the beginning of this chapter; Maple syrup? Substance is authenticity. I do believe that is what others need from us. Others are looking for those who they can depend on; persons that they are able to trust. We all need people that we believe are solid. Individuals that we can turn to who we are confident are authentic. One's that we can count on. That was the Maple syrup that came from real Maple trees in the Mohawk valley, New York. If you wanted the real thing, you could count on it. It wasn't artificial. We cannot let our lives become like my taste in pancake syrup became. I was so well adjusted to the fake artificial stuff that I wanted no part in what was authentic, real Maple syrup.

I think there are a lot of aspects in this world that we have lost sight of what was true in order to have what was convenient. I have always believed in God. I have always believed in salvation through Jesus. However, as I got into my high school and college years, the truths of the Bible didn't fit what I wanted to do. Therefore, what wasn't true became my truth; to justify what I wanted in my life. Living and doing whatever I wanted became my truth. After college, getting so far away from truth, I forgot truth. I started believing what wasn't truth; what was authentic. I started believing that as long as I did well (in my eyes) I would be alright. I would get to Heaven. That helped me change my thought on that very subject. I became very skeptical and cynical of Christianity. I began to question that there could only be one way to Heaven. How hypocritical, there are all these other religions; what makes Christianity the only way? I became antagonistic. I had been so immersed in what I wanted truth to be that I got blinded by counterfeit. This was continuing as my wife and I began to go to church.

Something we both had not done since before college. I would be cynical listening to sermons.

I had believed at an early age that Jesus had died for my sins; that he paid the price for my salvation. Here I was years later getting lost in what the world believed. Then a patient and loving God spoke to me in a very convicting way. It shook me. Like Paul getting the scales taken from his eyes so that he could see truth, so did I. I regained authenticity.

The bottom line is that we can have a lot of artificial flavors in our life and we don't even know it. You hear about someone who has a near death experience. That which flashes through their minds; that which is real and of value in their lives. Authentic. It is sad that we would have to have that to wake us up to it. Why not now? Why not take time, sit back and reflect? Truly, what are the things in my life that are just pudding? Am I putting too much into it at the expense of the authentic things/ persons in my life? Who am I affecting? What can I do to make changes; real changes?

The suggestion I make is prayer. First and foremost; let God tell you. And allow Him, by being still and listening; day in and day out, give you clarity.

Honesty with oneself and discipline is an ingredient of living a life of excellence.

CHAPTER 6

LIE DRESSED IN TRUTH'S CLOTHES

Growing up on the Jersey Shore I would spend much time during the summer at the Asbury Park boardwalk. My brother, sisters and I would venture the whole stretch from 7th avenue down through Convention Hall down to the south end to Paramount Theater. It was almost magical there in the 70's. Down on that boardwalk was the arcade where the pinball machines were. Back then, pinball machines were very popular. Someone always seemed to be playing while two others would squeeze between the sides to watch. The more action and color, the more alive the artistry on the machine, the more it got played. Inside the machine was its own world with bumpers and flippers. There were places where the ball seemed to sink into a hole only to pop out seconds later. The pinball itself had no control over itself. The ball was at the mercy of the individual player who was smacking the ball around registering points off of different bumpers. The player could manipulate the ball and direct it to hit certain places for points and ricochet off the wall and fly to the other side tallying more points. As the player became more focused he would press and push the machine to coerce the ball to play right where the player wanted it. I remember the ball zinging in every direction and seeing points being added. The ball would shoot off the walls and down and around and still be kept in play. With all the lights and sounds a pinball machine was a mini circus underneath the glass. Pinball games can be fun; that is, fun for the player.

Not fun for this ball as it side swiped the steel bumpers.

No control, no fun. She was in such a place as this; out of control. This steel pinball was her car. The car came to a stop; two small children looking down on her. "I need help."

Kim Dibiase, at that time Kim Youngman, was not in control. She will tell you that being the pinball wasn't any fun. Her car had bounced off the very real bumpers, side swiping cars. She had lost control of her car. She had lost control of her life. Unlike the pinball game, this wasn't a game that you could easily put down.

Kim's response to the children asking her if she was alright, "I need help." Frozen in time, Kim sat there. How did she end up here? Like a pinball that has no control, so was Kim. I remember Kim very well from our days in junior high school and high school. She was so vibrant and full of life. Here she was helpless, in need. How, again, did she end up here? In a little parking lot with her two back tires junked up because of her bumper car driving, is where she found herself. She found herself lost. When did she slip off the path of direction? Why, now, at 19 years old does she find her life careening out of control?

My middle daughter, Lilli, 8 years old, brought home a little ceramic flower pot filled with soil. In class, that day, the students were learning about plants and flowers. They were learning what makes them grow and how. They each received one of these ceramic pots filled with soil and planted a flower seed in it. They were given instructions when to water the plant and how much. Also, they were to put it by the window sill so that it could be exposed to sunlight. My daughter was very excited as she spoke so excitingly about this flower that was about to grow. With great anticipation she went to bed that night. There she was, though, the next morning downcast. I asked her what was wrong and without saying a word she pointed to the window sill. I walked over to her pot. I looked at it and asked her what was wrong. She said that she must have done something wrong and it died. She said this because she didn't see anything come out of the soil. All that she saw was dirt. There wasn't a flower. It didn't work. She watered it and put it by the sill the day before and nothing to show. I had to explain to her that when you plant a seed it first builds roots. The roots are underneath the buried seed. The roots will grow down and seek the water that is beneath it to grow and strengthen the seed that would flourish into a beautiful flower that would be seen atop the soil. In full view it is at first easy to point out and describe the results of what took place in the unseen, under the soil. Eventually whatever is being produced under the soil will manifest itself in the open.

> "For there is nothing hidden which will not
> be revealed, nor has anything been kept
> secret but that it should come to light."
> – Mark 4:22

For Kim there were seeds sown at a young age that she wasn't even aware of. These seeds were nurtured and cultivated that birthed strong roots that dug down and satisfied their thirst to spring up and out of the soil. The seed broke ground and reared its head. Kim grew up in an environment that drugs and alcohol were seen as normal. It was a culture that she grew into that in time the seeds sown wrought fruit of it. If it was normal then it was seen as true living to her. Kim lacked true identity. Now, she has true identity. She has also come to the truth that her life isn't hers to control. It is God's. But God allows us to choose Him or go our own way. Kim first chose to go her own way and God allowed her, knowing that it was at peril. But God also knew that He would be there at Kim's darkest moment and would give her strength to choose Him. God put a mature Christian in Kim's path to lead her to The Truth. This woman is an example of someone being obedient to living a life of excellence and passing it on. Passing it on to Kim. In choosing Him is where she began to find her real identity; her true identity. She knows who she is, Whose she is and in Whom she is. Her identity is in Christ Jesus. That wasn't always the case. When one doesn't know who they are then they are open to allow others, the world, dictate to them who they are. We falsely believe we are something we are not. We crave to be someone we weren't called to be because it looks cool or easy on the outside. However, after awhile it will lose its flavor or it will get us in a whole lot of trouble.

When we know who we are we are able to avoid, ignore and reject what we are not. Kim wasn't able to do that when she was younger because she had no idea who she was. Therefore she allowed the culture around her that seemed to be the norm to define her. She began to be someone she wasn't intended to become. This distinction took on life in how she saw herself and what she believed was for her and what she didn't need.

> "The thief does not come except to steal, and to kill, and to destroy. I have come that they may have life, and that they may have it more abundantly." – John 10:10

This scripture was the central theme of my first book and I have used it a few times in this book. It is a strong truth. There really is a God and there really is a fallen angel, Satan. We are told in the Bible that we are to be "sober, be vigilant; because your adversary the devil walks about like a roaring lion, seeking whom he may devour." – 1 Peter 5:8

In the chapter Predestination; It's Your Choice I talk about how the first part of John 10:10 is God's will. It is His predestination for you. He wants your life to be filled with an overflow of joy. The devil, your enemy, hates you. Why? It is because he wanted to be God. He was prideful and in that pride wanted to be God. We are created in God's image (Genesis 1:26). Therefore the enemy hates us. He attempts to ruin our lives by keeping us distracted from God's purposes in our lives. He does that by disguising lies with truth. No one, Kim or anyone desires to have the consequences of destructive behavior. No one starts living a certain lifestyle believing it is destructive. And that is how the Devil steals, kills and destroys, and we must be cognizant of this as we are told in the 1 Peter passage.

A brother of mine in ministry, Johnny Shelton, former NFL player who is the Chaplain for the Virginia Tech football team has recently told this story at a football camp we were working. The story of Truth and Lie. Truth and Lie skip school and go skinny dipping with a couple of lady friends. They were kicking it up having a fun time when Truth began to feel convicted that they were doing wrong. Truth swam over to where his clothes were and they were gone, just as Lie was as well. Truth, in his birthday suit, started thinking of what he could do since he was far from home. Truth remembered that Lie had a friend who lived close by and figured that is where Lie went to. Lies friend's name was deception. Truth, as inconspicuous as he could, quickly got to deception's house and banged on the door. Lie came to the door and was wearing Truth's clothes. Truth asked for his clothes back and Lie refused. Lie refused to acknowledge that they were Truth's clothes. Lie said that the clothes he had on were his own and the two of them started to get into a heated verbal argument. The argument drew attention from the neighbors who ended up calling the police. The police showed up and had to choose who to believe; the one who was clothed in truth or the one who was buck-naked. The police and the neighbors are like the world around us. They have been duped to believe a lie that is wrapped in truth. On the surface it would make sense. All they see is what would be the truth; blinded from the buck-naked truth right before them. The Word of God is the buck-naked truth. And it is very inconvenient and offensive to many people. However it is Truth. It is more convenient to twist and manipulate it to make it fit your own life than to have a Creator God who knows exactly what is best for you. That is Lie in Truth's clothes. And there are so many who are blinded by it. Also, many want

to say they believe in God, but on their own
see that not only in our culture but in churc
The buck-naked truth needs no posturing or
exceptions. There isn't negotiating to make
own life. But, that is indeed what the devil has been so
successful in being wrapped in distorted truth. (Lower
case t.) Deceptions house is exactly where Lie does his
impersonation that so many end up falling for. And the
devil is able to steal, kill and destroy someone's life as
well as have an adverse affect on those around them. Kim
can identify with allowing disguised lie to convince her it
was truth for her life.

In Kim's own words:

> I was living a very limited existence
> thinking this was truly all there was. I
> would turn to worldly answers while
> waiting for the magical peace to come over
> me. In Alcoholics Anonymous there is a
> saying that "insanity is repeating the same
> mistakes and expecting different results." I
> did not know the repetition of my mistakes.
> I was living a life of limitation. I was white
> knuckling life. I believed that this is how
> everyone lived. God showed me through
> spiritual awakening of a car crash that there
> was clearly a void that would never be filled
> through self medicating. I was given a new
> way to live. It was contrary to the lies that
> I had based my every choice on. It was as if
> I was waking up every day to a grey world.
> Suddenly everything was vibrant. I had a

choice for the first time in my life. I chose the vibrancy that suddenly made sense."

She chose God.

"For I know the thoughts that I think toward you, says the Lord, thoughts of peace and not of evil, to give you a future and a hope." – Jeremiah 29:11.

God knows the plans that He has for you. Each day that you wake up you must realize that the enemy has a purpose for you as well. John 10:10 tells us that exactly; Jesus wants to fulfill you and the Devil wants to deplete you. You will be under the control of one or the other. Jesus tells us that if we abide in Him and His teachings that we will come to know the truth and the truth will set us free. (John 8:31) Freedom from allowing people, circumstances, situations, feelings and emotions dictate our words, actions and decisions. We are told in Romans 8:12 that we do not have to give in to our sinful impulses. We do not have to heed to the suggestions that the enemy keeps putting in our ear. He is telling us those lies that are so conveniently wrapped in truth through deception. The devil had Kim believe those deceptions as truth for her life. It brought her to a place that the devil was succeeding in stealing, killing and destroying her life. He was controlling the pinball (Kim) flipping her all around banging off the bumpers of life that were taking a toll on her and she had no control over it. But, praise to God, that truth of God came to reveal the lie's of Kim's life. As Kim fed the truth into her life; that she is special, uniquely made by God, gifted, forgiven, redeemed, accepted, adopted, restored, replenished, cleansed and victorious, she began to have a paradigm shift in how she saw herself. She wasn't defeated. She wasn't hopeless. She wasn't too far gone. She had a redeemer who not only forgave her of her sins but gave her the power over them.

> "Bless the Lord, O my soul,
> And forget not all His benefits:
> Who forgives all your iniquities,
> Who heals all your diseases,
> Who redeems your life from destruction,
> Who crowns you with lovingkindness and
> tender mercies,
> Who satisfies your mouth with good things,
> So that your youth is renewed like the
> eagle's" – Psalm 103:2-5

Many people will tell you that they do not want to be under anyone's control. More and more the lie that wears truth's clothing becomes not only more and more real, but a lot more convenient and easier to fit into how they want to live their lives. And God gives them that free will to choose. However, living a life outside of God's parameters and choosing to do whatever you want is really being under the control of the devil. Someone who says that they will do whatever they want whenever they want isn't really free. From the fall of Adam and Eve we know that we all inherited sin. In that sin the devil can control us by getting us to act on our feelings and emotions. Someone who is addicted, whether it is alcohol, drugs; legal or illegal, pornography, gambling, sex, etc isn't free. They are not choosing, but are in bondage to sin. This is the Devil destroying people, marriages and families which lead to the destruction of the fabric of the stability of our communities and nation. It is exactly the enemies plan and it seems to be working. However, as you have read about Kim, God is a redeemer and can bring out of the depths of devastation a life abundant. He loves each one of us so much that He would send His Son to die for us, that we not only would live a life abundant, but to live it eternally never separated from Him.

God does love everyone He has created. He created us to share in who He is: love. However God is Holy and sin cannot be in his presence. When you have breathed your last on this Earth you must be holy and righteous without sin to come into God's presence forever: Heaven. If you are not, you will be eternally separated from God in a torment that our minds cannot comprehend: hell. How can anyone go to Heaven then? "For all have sinned and fall short of the glory of God." – Romans 3:23 and "the wages of sin is death" – Romans 6:23a.

Therefore the answer is no one can. That is, not on their own doing. That is where the marvelous grace of God comes in.

> "For God so loved the world that He gave His only begotten Son, that whoever believes in Him should not perish but have everlasting life." – John 3:16

> "For He made Him who knew no sin to be sin for us, that we might become the righteousness of God in Him"
> – 2 Corinthians 5:21

"But God, who is rich in mercy, because of
His great love with which He loved us, even
when we were dead in trespasses, made us
alive together with Christ (by grace you
have been saved)" – Ephesians 2:4-5

"That if you confess with your mouth the Lord Jesus
and believe in your heart that God has raised Him from
the dead, you will be saved" – Romans 10:9. Saved from
what? Saved from the wrath of God that is on anyone
who comes before God with sin and then subjected to
eternal life apart from God.

"Yet in all these things we are more than
conquerors through Him who loved us."
– Romans 8:37

This is good news! We do not have to live under
condemnation. We do not have to feel that we are no
good or have done such horrible things that we cannot
be forgiven; that we cannot receive peace. That is a lie
that the devil wants you to think. He wants you to think
that you can't help it or that everyone sins a little and
as long as I do good things I am going to Heaven. He
wants you to think that a loving God would never send
anyone to Hell. A loving God doesn't and that is why He
has made a way, even though we can't, to be free from
sin. The last verse from Romans 8:37 is some more great
news. Not only can we be made to have peace with God
and our sins forgiven but He also gives us power to grow
strong and live abundant lives; to live a life of excellence!
Someone say Amen!

When I first asked Kim to share her story about overcoming her struggles I wasn't quite sure where it would lead but knew God did. I wrote the first couple of pages and then went blank. I let this chapter sit for a couple of months and then began to pray for God to reveal its overall purpose. The purpose is that I know that not everyone reading this chapter is a Christian. And some that are can relate to feeling like an out of control pinball being tossed back and forth. There are stories that may seem worse than Kim's; right in the Bible! What great hope we have when we can look in the Word and see destructive people being redeemed from defeat to victory. If you are reading this and feel hopeless know that the enemy wants you to drown on that belief, however, God is the life preserver, the person bringing you into the boat. Believe that His Word is truth and just cry out to Him for help. He's knocking on the door waiting for you to let Him in. He loves you. Let Him love all over you.

This is what Kim did and now passes it on to her husband and her children, who are being encouraged to live a life of excellence in Him.

CHAPTER 7

CREATION

Stars in the sky
birds flying by.
Mice scamper and scurry
while deer run and hurry.
Rabbits hop and jump around
worms squirm underground.
Wolves howl
when cats are on the prowl.
Tree's so high
mountains touch the sky.
Fish in the seas
honey made by bee's.
From the land to the ocean
all of creation is in motion.

– Arianna Treppel, 10 years old

CHAPTER 8

INDELIBLE

Indelible Blue. That is a name of a company that I worked for in Raleigh, 1995, did business with. They had a really cool logo. It was one that I would always remember, even now, 15 years later. It made such an impression on me that I was curious what that word meant; indelible. It meant exactly the affect it was having on me. Webster says that indelible is "a mark not easily erased or washed away; Incapable of being destroyed."

Our life is full of indelible moments. For my parent's generation, without a doubt, is remembering exactly where they were when they heard that President Kennedy had been shot. For my generation and all that were alive in 2001 would obviously be 9/11, the terrorist attacks on our country. I will never forget where I was when the first plane hit the towers. I was, of all places, a television repair store waiting to pick up our TV set that was there for service. As I waited the clerk pointed to the television sets on in the store, some 2 dozen, all on different channels, all showing the same thing; a second plane hitting the other tower. The whole day, the emotions, the phone calls, the conversations, the feelings; would never be erased, can never be water downed. I remember every part of the day as if it were yesterday. I can tell you nothing about 3 days before. Not even the day before. But of everything on that Tuesday, September 11, 2001 is crisp in my mind; who I talked to, where I was, where I went. I am sure it is the same for you. It left an indelible mark on each of us. Unfortunately, worse on some than others who lost family and/or friends. Even as time went by, years now, it has left an indelible mark. It will be with us forever.

I remember my first grade teacher, Miss Mika. Even though it has been 34 years since I have been in first grade, I still remember so much of that year to this day. Some of the moments I can recall pretty specifically. There was, though, one time that she spoke to me that had a lasting impact on my life; an indelible impact. Our class was learning how to write words from singular to plural. I know this sounds crazy to remember this, but, well, I do. I wrote down the word lady and then its plural ladies. Ms. Mika came over my shoulder as I was doing my assignment and whispered to me that I got it right. That she was very proud of me and that I was doing a great job. Do you think she remembers? Probably not. Of course she has had 100's of students over the years. I had only one first grade teacher. Here is the point that I want to make. This a marker in my life that I carry with me to this day and had given me such encouragement that subconsciously and consciously I see myself as one that can succeed. In which has helped me discover that I have gifts and abilities to be a blessing to others. That I can contribute to other's lives. There is no doubt in my mind that it was an ingredient that has been part of the makeup of who I am. She had sowed a seed of empowerment into my life. It was a foundation builder for my life. This was added to others throughout the years that have brought me to a point that I can go onto a stage in front of an auditorium of people and confidently speak to them about living an abundant life. Speaking to them about sowing into lives of those who they come in contact with. Indelibly. What is important here is how subtle, simple the words spoken had an impact on me that I remember 3+ decades later. Think about the words that you use each day. We say words so flippantly; but how long lasting they can be. Are your words and actions constructive or deconstructive? Do you realize the power you have to be an influence, both good and bad, in lives of others?

A man comes onto a stage to speak to a large audience. The architecture of the hall that he is speaking in is unavoidably noticeable. There are huge beautiful columns. There is glass all around the sides from floor to very high ceilings. Outside it is cold and stormy. Inside is warm and inviting due to the comfortable seats and perfectly placed rows on a perfect decline towards the stage. This gentleman points out how blessed they are to be inside from all the yucky weather outside. He begins to point out the array of stunning creativity that the architect had woven together that is not only incredibly beautiful but is strategically mastered that every seat has a great view and the acoustics are harmonious. After a moment he asked the crowd, rhetorically, when do you think the architect had brought together this masterpiece of an auditorium into her imagination that would become what it is today? 5 years ago? 10, 15? No, he tells the audience. It was when she was about 4 years old. See, when she was just a little girl she took out some crayons and used her imagination that comes with a four year old, and drew a picture. It was a masterpiece.

With a smile on her face and pride in her voice she ran to her father to show him the picture. Now as he looked at it he saw scribble with no obvious pattern or any visible order. Only colors going every which way. But her father looked with great delight and told her what a great job she did. He patiently, with his attention fixed on her, listened as she described the picture that she had made. He could see it all and he told her so. He was so proud of the work she did. And because it made her feel so good to please her father she went back and made more and more pictures for him. And more and more he solidified her belief in herself. She connected her drawing pictures with success and fulfillment. She would draw, paint, anyway to make pictures for she loved to do it because her father so much blessed her with his adulation and pleasure in the work she did. As she got older he confirmed in her, her desire to take drawing classes which lead to drafting classes and eventually architectural school. And because of this, he told the crowd, we are the beneficiaries of her blessings.

Then the man on stage asked everyone to turn to the side and look out the window. Look over there. How would you like it if we got to spend our evening in that great place? The people were a little perplexed for all they saw out the window was the woods. See, he told them, there isn't another greatly crafted auditorium. There isn't another great creative imaginative architect. There isn't, because that seed was ripped out of the soil before it could even take root. It was ripped out because of negativity, because of apathy. There was a mother or father who didn't have the time to look at some scribble on a 4 year old's paper. They didn't have time for silliness. They might have even pointed out to her that they were sloppy and coloring outside the lines. These are the persons that the child looks to for approval, for love. A child's budding dream ending before it got started. A child who grows up with the continual hesitation and self doubt because it was confirmed in her by someone who might of not had any idea the indelible mark they made on her when their derogatory comments, or even worse, lack of interest at all, took away her ambition.

We have been given a very powerful tool. We have the power to be constructive or destructive in another's life. What we say. How we say it. Or what we fail to say or do to bless someone else. And just as nitrogen oxide can be used to save someone's heart or be an ingredient to make a bomb, so too do we have the ability to build up or destroy. What are the indelible marks that you are leaving today? How about tomorrow?

I want to share with you a marker in my life that had a profound, indelible impact on me. Two years ago I had the opportunity to go up to New York, with some coworkers in ministry with the Fellowship of Christian Athletes, to see a couple of Yankee games on the last home stand of the original Yankee stadium. We would drive up from Raleigh and go straight to Yankee Stadium on a Friday night for the first game and then the Saturday afternoon game the next day. A friend of ours, Lee Rouson, who works with FCA as well, had hooked us up with a friend of his who owned a parking garage in Manhattan that would give us a free place for our van to stay while we took the subway to the Bronx. After the game we were going to crash at Lee's house and then get up the next day, go to the game and then back on the road. Well, we drove all day Friday and as we hit

Jersey we also hit the rain and cool temperatures. And of course, traffic on the turnpike. (Imagine that, traffic on the NJ turnpike. Actually, you don't have to, it's a reality.) OK, moving on. We get up to Manhattan and get to Lee's friend's parking garage. That helped out tremendously. We take the train to Yankee stadium. It is cold and rainy and after a couple hours of rain delay the game is postponed to a double header the next day. So here we are, wet and tired, having to take the train back to Manhattan. Get the van out of the parking garage and head to Jersey where we will be staying at Lee's house. We get to Lee's house close to 11pm. We have been at it since early that morning driving 10+ hours just to get to Manhattan. Trains, planes and automobiles. So now, we show up at Lee's house where he is waiting up for us while his wife and children are upstairs sleeping. What I am thinking is that Lee is going to say hi, point to where we can crash, start heading upstairs and without turning around waving his hand and say he will see us in the morning. We really couldn't blame him if he did. It would be understandable. He was doing us a great favor by not only letting us stay at his house but hooking us up with his friend's parking garage. We didn't have to pay for a place to stay and, if you could only know how much it costs to park in a Manhattan garage, no charge to park; a great blessing in its own. We truly were blessed by Lee just right there. Well, we get to Lee's and Lee comes to the door, greets us, and leads us to the kitchen. He has a couple brownie pans out and the coffee machine and some other snacks. Lee has us sit down and begins to take our orders. He brings out soda and juices, fruit and cookies. He makes coffee and offers other snacks. He waits on us and makes sure that we have all we need. After we hang out for a little while he leads us to a couple of different rooms set up with blankets and pillows. I was in awe of his hospitality. Here is Lee Rouson, 2 time Super Bowl champion with the New York Giants, serving us at midnight.

We get to bed after midnight and we plan to get up early enough to go to the city. I sleep on a couch in the basement, which is more of a game room. It is a real nice set up with a full bath. I get up early, to get a head start, and take a shower before heading upstairs. Towels and wash clothes were folded and on the sink when I went into the bathroom. They weren't there the night before. After I get dressed I go upstairs and Lee is again, as if he never left from just hours before, in the kitchen. He has coffee a percolating. He has two different coffee cakes coming out of the oven. He has fruit sliced up and spread on a serving platter. He has eggs and bacon set out on the table. And he greets us, as we stroll in, singing. I am floored. Man, I thought I was a morning person. It is one thing to be up early after a late night, but to also to get up to make a whole bunch of breakfast for others is the truest example of servitude that I have experienced. His wife and children were still upstairs and sleeping but Lee was showing me the example of serving with joy. He seemed so happy to see us blessed. To see us enjoy a good breakfast.

It had been quite a few years since I have been to a Yankee game. Even though I had been back to New York a few times since I moved to North Carolina, I was excited about going up to see the Yankees play two in the old stadium. That Saturday after leaving Lee's house we took the PATH into New York and took the subway to the lower west side to Ground Zero. I had been there the year before but it was still a trip I looked forward to going with these guys. And then the thrill of seeing a Yankee doubleheader. But the most profound impact the trip had on me was Lee's hospitality. That Lee went so far out of his way to make us feel real comfortable and to leave not in want. So, our 2 day trip to New York had a very indelible impact on me. It wasn't the games or Ground Zero, but Lee's desire to make sure we were taken care of. It has inspired me to be so much more conscious to think serving others first. I have since spent some time with Lee and have told him how much it meant to me and that it has challenged me to be more selfless and other people focused. What I took from that time with Lee is that living the life of excellence takes a lifestyle of taking it off you and putting it on others. Being God centered, other people focused takes some cultivating. Our natural man is selfish; each and every one of us. Our flesh wants to be satisfied and is always looking out for King Self. In order to take the focus of one self and to serve others you must be self assured. Have you ever been around someone who was so smooth, didn't ever seem rattled and was always making sure everything was cool with you? The kind of person you would want to be in the foxhole with. Or better yet, in a boat during a storm.

> "But as they sailed He fell asleep. And a windstorm came down on the lake, and they were filling with water, and were in jeopardy. And they came to Him and awoke Him, saying," Master, Master, we are perishing!" Then He arose and rebuked the wind and the raging of the water. And they ceased, and there was a calm."
> – Luke 8:23-24.

Jesus was continually being challenged and discredited by the ruling religious authority. Wherever He went they followed Him scheming to see how they could trap Him; to get him to contradict Himself. One time, Jesus answered them saying that He knew where He came and He knew where He was going. He knew His identity and His purpose. Do you know yours? Just as I am writing this my middle daughter, Lilli, came downstairs, head down with a sad look on her face. "Arianna (our oldest) said that I am not smart." My wife, Marlies, looked at Lilli and asked her," Do you believe that?" Lilli answered, "No." Lilli allowed someone else to make her uncertain of herself but was reinforced by her mother of what she should be certain of. There are two things here to look at. First; when you are brought to a place of doubt, do you stop and reassess the certainty that it exists? Second; are you one who helps stabilize someone in their assurance? In my first book *Live the Life Abundant* I have a chapter titled "Who God Says You Are." It is important to know who your Creator says that you are. First and foremost it is that you are uniquely and specially made with gifts and talents. We cannot allow other people, circumstances, situations, feelings and emotions dictate our words actions and decisions. We are able to when we gain strong footing on the solid rock of truth. A truth that doesn't change regardless of what popular opinion believes for the day, but stands the test of time. We too shall be assured. Our confidence becomes, not in ourselves, but in Almighty God. And as we grow in our faith, and in our trust, we grow in that confidence and assurance, which are not easily swayed. As we become solid in who we are we don't need reckoning, applaud or acknowledgement. We can become so sure of ourselves, in Him, that we are able to focus and serve others and be blessed because of it. The enemy tries to discourage you in thinking that you must take care of yourself, look out for yourself. You become less effective for God to shine through you when you become preoccupied with self preservation. We grow more in excellence when we encourage and lift up others towards excellence.

> "Let nothing be done through selfish ambition or conceit, but in lowliness of mind let each esteem others better than himself. Let each of you look out not only for his own interests, but also for the interests of others." – Philippians 2:3-4

I have had a hard time laying down my megaphone at times. You know, when you feel the world needs to know what you have accomplished or how much you went out of the way to make something happen for someone else. I have to fight back saying "you're welcome!" loudly and a bit sarcastically when I stand and wait with the door open to allow someone to walk in and they do not one bit make any gesture to acknowledge the great deed I just did for them. Not only do I want them to know but I have it in mind to let someone else know. I might just want to call my 10 closest friends and let them know how I went out of my way for this ungrateful person. But, I thank God, that as He has been so patient in working on me, that my own personal reckoning is dissipating more and more. I am learning that God alone is my sufficiency and do not need reckoning. In that, it allows me to be other people focused a lot more. In place of the need to boast I have peace of contentment of whose I am.

"Therefore humble yourselves under the mighty hand of God, that He may exalt you in due time." – 1 Peter 5:6

God used Lee in such a powerful way. The indelible mark that it made on me is motivation to serve others, to be a champion for others that they may be encouraged to strive forward and be all they can be; to live a life of excellence. Living a life that pulls people up instead of putting people down is what we need more examples of. In a world that teaches you to look after number one it is refreshing and inspiring to see someone put others before themselves and will lead others to do so as well.

Be honest with yourself. Are you assured in yourself that you are satisfied with someone else being lifted up? Do you trust God to take care of your needs that you can focus on others to fulfill their needs? Do you have a Lee Rouson in your life that you can emulate that you can serve someone in such a way that it moves them to do the same?

Living a Life of Excellence is first sowing into other's lives that they feel emboldened to live a life of excellence. It will leave a mark. An indelible one.

CHAPTER 9

ARE YOU DUMBED DOWN?

My eight year old had a challenge on her hand and I was going to lead, motivate, and guide and see her through to triumph. I would see her take something that seemed too hard to do and learn that indeed with concentration and determination she would overcome a hindrance that she became accustomed to yielding to and rationalizing that she was doing the best she could and the results were the results and it would suffice. Hey, it is the world we live in and some things are the way they are and that is the way it is. It is what it is. (How many times have you heard that saying the last couple of years?) However I wasn't going to let my daughter Lilli succumb to defeat. She would persevere. Yes she would and from it she will learn that she can "do hard things" and grow in her belief in herself. I truly believed she could make peanut butter and jelly (with Fluff) sandwich without having jelly all over the kitchen counter. Now, I know what you're thinking; a little over the top there buddy. Of course it is only to make a point. Kids stuff? Exactly. I am dealing with a kid. And this is a great time for her to learn a lesson on being able, even when she doesn't want to, to do hard things. For as we know kids stuff turns into adult stuff. If she doesn't learn it now she will have such a harder, more difficult time, as an adult dealing with tough situations. Because of what she experiences now will have an impact on her future experiences in how she sees her ability, or lack of, in a given situation. It was a great opportunity for her to be able to see herself able to be successful in something she was having trouble with. So first we started with not putting the jelly bottle upside down and trying to time the avalanche of jelly coming out of the bottle and her whipping the jar back right side up. As you can imagine, way too much jelly and it flying out on the counter top when she flipped the bottle back up. This child of mine eats pb&j quite frequently so I felt we needed to remedy this. Super dad to the rescue. I was able to get her to leave the bottle right side up and use a spoon to get her jelly out since it would slide right off the knife. And we would get less each time so that it wouldn't spill all over the place. It seemed to be working. She saw that she could do it. A little more practice and she would have a clean, neat work area. I limbered up and stretched before I patted myself on the back. The next week, after my wife came back from food shopping, Lilli comes rushing to me with a smile on her face. "Daddy, daddy! Look; mommy bought jelly in a squeeze bottle!" Oh, I was so excited for her. I kind of sighed, shook my head, and smiled. My little lesson on tackling hard things had been wiped away by convenience in a bottle.

I am to be very careful what I write next since my wife will be reading this. IT MOST CERTAINLY ISN'T MY WIFE'S FAULT that Lilli's development is being studded. OK, that is a little much. But, in all honesty, it is the powerful machine called advertisement. We are continually bombarded with suggestions that we aren't capable of being able to handle tasks and therefore need help from companies that are at the ready to save us from ourselves. I saw consecutive commercials that showed both how inept I am and that I should do something about it. The first commercial showed a woman at her kitchen sink. It was time to do the dishes and she had the liquid dishwashing soap in a plastic bottle and the sponge in the other hand. The very easy task of popping up the top of the bottle to allow the free flow of soap became an incredible hassle. Then as she turned the bottle to squirt some out onto the sponge it went all over! Kind of like grape jelly missing the bread and going all over the counter top. This woman was beside herself. I am sure she doesn't have time for this and cannot and will not subject herself anymore to being incompetent. Scratch that, it isn't her incompetency but the inferior tools to clean dishes. She shouldn't put up with it anymore. Thank heavens for the new product on the market to save her. This would make a dramatic impact on her life. One that brings fulfilling happiness to a life that might be lacking in the happy department. She would get the upright dishwashing liquid dispenser that had sensors to release just the right amount of dishwashing liquid at just the right speed. Now, this woman would only have to put the sponge under the little plastic nozzle and she would have a utopian experience that would lead to a great dishwashing experience and a relaxing rest of the day.

The next commercial had someone who was making a huge mess and about to lose it. This person couldn't crack an egg without it running down her arm, the floor, and the counter top. They would try another one and another one; exasperating, that is, to watch. Who can help this person so they wouldn't have to deal with being traumatized and the now to be ever present belief of inferiority? No fear, the perfect product is here. It is a upright thing a magigger that you put an egg in and it cracks it with perfection.

Now, I know the first thing you are thinking is where can you get these two products; they're awesome. And that you already buy the jelly in the squeeze bottle. As you know, so now we have one in our refrigerator. Along with these two helpful dandies are many other products that enable us to not have to do. Believe me, I don't want to go back in time and live without AC, TV, ESPN and the likes. However, when convenience becomes an enabler and keeps you from having to work at overcoming and achieving it is a detriment and can keep you from living a life of excellence. Come on, an egg breaker and soap dispenser? No, it isn't the products, it is the belief that we need things to take place of our own God given ability to strive forward and excel. If we aren't continually challenged we lose our edge. When I first started our business I had challenges everyday from all different directions. But because I didn't have any help I had to figure things out and get them solved. I didn't have a choice. No alternatives.

But now there are so many alternatives. The easier road is made available. If there isn't an incentive to strive to achieve then why strive? If you are continued to be enabled and do not have to find what is in you than how can you ever find out what you have? How many times have you heard of individuals who had to work out everything, every angle, with perseverance and drive just to survive a situation? And what does the person say? They say that they didn't realize how much courage, strength, ingenuity, spunk that they had. They find out they have more to themselves when they are stretched and have to dig down. Isn't that when you find out what you are made of? But if someone or something continues to do it for you it will sap your motivation to empowerment. One of the things that bother me about politicians promising so much for people is that people lose their own ambition and individual determination. It is very healthy for a person to have to use their God given abilities to excel and overcome and be victorious. A sense of accomplishment will change a person's attitude about themselves in an empowering way that isn't only beneficial to them but also to others. But if someone is always making it easy for you than you start depending on them than on yourself. Then we expect others to do for us, and in turn, we give them power over us. We compromise and become conditioned to believe that we can't, they can, and they become our master. This country that we live in became great because so many individuals were steadfast in the conviction that with hard work and determination they could achieve.

> "I know how to be abased, and I know how to abound. Everywhere and in all things I have learned both to be full and to be hungry, both to abound and to suffer need. I can do all things through Christ who strengthens me." – Philippians 4:12-13

One way that we get duped, to get dumbed down, is believing that our circumstances and situations are just too hard. We learn how to make excuses of why we aren't able. We justify that it is because we don't have this or that or because we have this or that. And with that we become more and more reliant on politicians, government and others. I see it all around, I see it with myself. We have so many outs in this society we live in that it becomes too easy to not sacrifice and put the nose to the grind stone and let someone else do it for you. And what happens is we believe in the rationalizations and justifications of compromising; of being dumbed down.

There was an American company that was negotiating with an Asian manufacturer to buy some of the Asian company's products. We will call the product widgets. (You understand if you ever took an accounting class.) The American company wanted to seem very strong and sharp. The negotiations came down to one stipulation. If it was agreed upon then they would have a deal. The American company was a very reputable company that had very high standards. In order for them to do business with this manufacturer the Asian company had to agree that there wouldn't be any more than 2% defectives on any shipment. The Asian company agreed. When the American company received the first shipment it came in one huge container and then another box a lot smaller than the container. With this first shipment came a letter. The letter stated that the big box was for the agreed amount of widgets and the second box was at the amount of 2% of the larger container. The smaller container contained the defective widgets. The letter stated they weren't sure why the company wanted defective widgets but that here they were. The American company had gotten used to defective widgets that it became the norm to expect and accept a certain amount. The trend became acceptable. "It is what it is." What it is, is being dumbed down. The Asian company didn't operate that way. There might be defective widgets that came off the assembly line but it was absolutely unacceptable that any of them would be shipped off to a customer. I most certainly am not making a blanket statement in regards to how companies from two different cultures operate. However, the point is that we, America and everywhere else for the matter, are allowing ourselves to be less than excellent and it is becoming the norm.

There are a lot of grape squeeze bottles in our life that are robbing us of the satisfaction of actualizing that life to the fullest.

We can't look around and blame companies, government or any other institution but we must look at ourselves individually. Each of us has our own mountains to conquest. We each need to do all we can where we are with what we have.

There is a sports writer in our local paper that was going to do a story on a group preparing for a triathlon. He was a former college baseball player who was just a few years removed from his playing days. But for him, just like me and so many others, the word triathlon evokes thoughts of ultra athletic hard core and crazy, grueling torture of the human body and mind. To ride a bike, swim and run all in one shot, for the distances they had, isn't on too many wish lists including this sports writer. He approached local individuals who train and compete in triathlons. He gave a new meaning to the term "not get personally involved" in a story you are putting together. However, he was persuaded to train with a local triathlon team. The first morning his alarm went off and it was pitch black outside. He was met with a challenge. This is a challenge, in general, that each of us face pretty much every day. It isn't easy to get up a lot earlier than you usually do. Your body is full out telling you how much comfortable and warm you are; nice and cozy in bed compared to a chilly uninviting dark outdoors. Each one of us has challenges each day to do hard things. It is here where we decide to be a champion; at the right time when we have every reason not to but do. He wasn't a competing athlete anymore. He was not ever one that did such strenuous training at this magnitude. He was done training. He was now married with a job. There was no longer a drive to be in good physical shape. But here he was deciding to do a "hard thing". He made a clear cut choice. He was going to go against his feelings and get up very early in the morning and train with this triathlon group. It was tough. He was tired. Hey, his intentions, anyway, were good. Like many, he most certainly could have kept hitting the snooze. But he forced himself to get up and get going. He would meet this group and see their positive energetic attitudes and it encouraged him. He thought they were insane to be so alive so early in the a.m., but it motivated him. He came to find out that he could push himself into better shape physically and mentally.

What are those things that are outside your comfort zone that you may have felt doing but when it came down to it; it just was too inconvenient, too much sacrifice, too much physical pain? It is one thing to say that you are going to get up at 5am and pray, go for a run or work out. It sounds good and you know that you can only benefit from it. However, it is a whole different story when the alarm clock goes off and all you hear is rain pelting the side of the house and you see nothing but pitch black. This is exactly what this sports writer was faced with. He, and we, must come to a point where we realize that those things that are going to carry us to improvement must be done. He has just completed his first triathlon. He feels energetic all the time. It has changed his outlook on himself and everything else around him. When we succeed at difficult things it enhances our belief in ourselves and expands our belief in what we can achieve. We accomplish one hard task we start looking to what else God is calling us to do that we turned a deaf ear to before. In my first book I spoke about how bad do you want it? I worked so hard and was able to become a starter on my college football team. It had a great impact on me. I do not believe I would talk in front of audiences, write books or be able to run a business if I didn't grow in confidence and in belief from persevering on the football field.

Don't let this world or past experiences keep you from being courageous to step up and do hard things.

> "There is no such thing as an average human being. If you have a normal brain, you are superior." – Dr. Ben Carson MD, Director of Neurosurgery, Johns Hopkins University

As a young kid Dr. Carson had every reason to be dumbed down and to accept it. His circumstances reinforced it as well as kids in his classes; not to mention his grades. Even at elementary grade age he was convinced that he was dumb. You could hardly blame him. His mother had only a third grade education and was 13 when she got married. When Ben was 8 his parents got divorced. His mom would work 2, 3 jobs. He and his brother fell farther and farther behind in school. By 5th grade he was labeled as a dummy that was violent with an uncontrollable temper. Now here is where society and his mom clash on how we see young Ben. Society, now, would put the kid gloves on and make sure Ben was in a class with kids more like himself who just didn't fit in the regular school mold. He would not be looked upon to excel and achieve. He doesn't have his father around and his life is too tough. Maybe in 15 years your taxes would make sure he had everything he needed because by then he would not be expected, therefore not by him either, to do much with his life. Well, that isn't how it worked out. Let me tell you how it did. His mother was working all the time. You would fully understand if she would allow the television to be her sitter, to be her children's counselor and life teacher. Being a single mom working more than 1 job would take up all her time and energy. One job she had was cleaning houses. The owner of one of the houses had a library with a vast collection of books. She asked the wealthy successful man if he had read all of the books. He scanned the shelves of books and replied that he indeed had. She put the connection together. Success = books. Books = success. Achieve, excel.

She wasn't going to allow Ben or his brother to settle anymore. They were no longer going to allow circumstances, situations, feelings, other people, dictate their lives anymore. She wasn't going to allow them to be dumbed down anymore. TV time got severely cut back. Ben's mother no longer allowed them to watch television or go out and play until all homework was complete. Then she required them to read two library books a week and hand in to her written reports about the books. Within a few weeks Ben's teacher brought to school rock samples. Ben recognized the rocks from one of the books he read and he identified them in front of the whole class. It was at that moment, before all those kids who had called him dummy, that he realized that he wasn't stupid. New found knowledge; new found confidence. How his life must have changed. Knowledge is power, and with this Ben's world opened up. He had got a new sense of purpose and determination. Within 1 year he went from the very bottom of his class to the top. He had now a strong hunger for knowledge and the rewards it brought. How he saw himself, and what he believed he could become, stretched higher and higher. He got to a point that he wanted to become a physician. He not only tapped the potential that he had but he also was able to learn to control his temper. He graduated high school with honors and attended Yale and earned a degree in Psychology. From there he went onto the University of Michigan. He discovered he had a high degree of hand/eye coordination which would help him excel in neurosurgery. By the age of 32 he became the Director of Pediatric Neurosurgery at Johns Hopkins University. 32! Maybe you could qualify at that age to be the director of your town's little league or your fantasy football league. But Director of Pediatric Neurosurgery? He must have been born with a stethoscope around his neck. Not quite. It wasn't even 20 years earlier he was labeled dumb with no aspirations to counter that assessment. The movie, *Gifted Hands*, starring Cuba Gooding Jr., is about Dr. Carson's remarkable life and him being the first physician to lead a team to successfully separate Siamese twins who were conjoined at the back of the head. In 2008 Dr. Carson was presented with the highly esteemed Presidential Medal of freedom. He devotes time to helping young people. How many Dr. Carson's will never materialize because they didn't have someone to interrupt their being dumbed down and believing it to be true.

I don't believe it's going to come from a president's big speech of promises; or any other politician or leader for that matter. I do believe that this country lifts itself back up by individuals who inspire, challenge and encourage people around them to strive to be more than they are and not to settle. Dr. Carson's mom could have just compromised and justified why her sons underachieved and acted the way they did. They were at such a disadvantage. She could have most certainly felt sorry for herself, but she didn't, she persevered. She did hard things (working 2-3 jobs) and expected her sons to do the same (read and report on 2 books a week). The habits we have really form a lifestyle that we become accustomed to. If you have a low thought of yourself and allow it to be reinforced by those things that you watch and hear and the people you surround yourself with it will perpetuate throughout your days and it becomes who you are. It is how you see yourself and how you act, speak and decide accordingly. Dr. Carson fought, complained and grumbled when his mom first restricted his comforts and forced him to step up and apply himself.

For the overwhelming majority of us, we need, at times for someone to be blatantly honest with us. We don't like it and might ignore or get defensive. However, if we are truly honest and open we should consider all encouragement that is challenging us to be, and do, more. Challenges are opportunities to find out what we are made of. In this dumbing down world, we need to know that we were made in the image of God. More than a few times in the Bible God has called on someone to step out of their comfort zone and scale higher heights; to do things they wouldn't ever think of doing or believing they could. Moses, Gideon, Jeremiah and Timothy are just a few that viewed themselves as a lot less than how God saw them. And that, I believe, is our biggest problem. We have allowed the culture we live in to define us instead of the God who created us. First we are taught that we are here just by chance, an end result of a long line of evolution from a tadpole. We are continually fed that our purpose is in getting; consuming. The result will be that we will be satisfied. In turn our mind-set has been manipulated from love, serving and contributing to one that becomes self centered on style instead of substance. We voluntarily give up the power that we hold to uplift, encourage and strengthen those around us and become subjected to doing as the media driven culture dictates.

A certain man traveled to Africa to meet a farmer at the farmer's property. When the man got to the farm he went around with the farmer and observed these huge powerful elephants pushing and pulling; getting the work done. The man just marveled at all the work these elephants accomplished during the day. As the day ended he and the farmer walked around to where the elephants laid down for rest and sleep for the night. He noticed that each elephant went to a post in the ground and would lay right next to it. The elephants would retire for the night not moving from the post. The man was dumbfounded. He asked the farmer," You don't have any fence, any way of restraining them. How do you know that the elephants won't just get up and leave?" The farmer explained to the man that when the elephants were babies they had a thick rope tied from the post to their legs. When the elephants were very young they weren't strong at all. At night they would try to get up and go but the rope held them up and after a while the elephants gave up. As the elephants got older the thickness of the rope would get smaller and smaller until the farmer didn't even use a rope. He didn't have to. The elephants have already been defeated in their mind. The rope wasn't needed anymore because the elephant has already been defeated. The rope has done its job. Though the rope isn't physically there the elephant doesn't believe that it can go anywhere. It is no longer the rope that keeps the elephant from getting up and going but itself. The elephant is convinced and therefore is resigned to the fact it lays next to the post each night for it has no other option.

Could not Ben Carson have been same way? Yes, he could of, but he had someone open his eyes to the fact that there was not anymore a rope to hold him back. That rope can represent many hindrances to our development of living a life of excellence, living a life of manifest destiny. It took taking that awareness of that truth and direction to walk away from the post. Walking away from poverty in more than one form; psychologically, mentally and/or physically. It took a determined mother to see her sons were not tied down to a post by a rope.

What are your perceived ropes?

Be honest with yourself. What is keeping you? Nightly TV line up? Have to watch certain shows? You know they aren't real, even the reality ones. Either way, it is taking time away from you actualizing that which you should and could be doing. Do you have accepted beliefs in yourself that were cemented years ago by circumstances, events, other people that has allowed you to be less than who you were created to be? Why don't you take time and write down some desires that are in your heart. Maybe there are some that are buried that might have to be uncovered. When you do this, do not justify why you can't but instead brainstorm what you would have to do. What sacrifices could you make; what choices could you make, that would enable you to achieve. Find out what is in you. Don't use your age, whether too young or too old. There are many life stories of individuals who didn't get started with their dreams until later in life. There are individuals who finally went to college and got their diplomas, others running their first road race, finishing high school, starting businesses, in their eighties.

Getting married!
Learned to surf.
Rebuilt a car engine.
Learned to read.
Wrote a book.
Found a long lost relative or friend.
Forgave someone.
Learned a foreign language.
Became a mentor.
Accepted Jesus as their Lord and Savior.
Quit smoking.
Quit drinking.
Started walking and lifting weights.
Started playing golf.
Volunteered to read at the public library.
Learned to paint.
Play the piano.
16 year olds sailing around the world. Solo!
18 year olds starting their own businesses.

Or a single mom who dropped out of school in middle school, could barely read, held at least 2 jobs and was determined to make sure that her two boys work hard and diligently to actualize the gifts that were put in them before they were even born. How great it is, that many people have been blessed by, when this woman did a hard thing. A very hard thing amid very hard circumstances to make sure her two boys lived a life of excellence. Ben's mom lived the epitome of living a life of excellence; she made certain her boys would. Who is counting on you to live a life of excellence? Who has God put in your life that you are to be a steward of excellence? I can tell you that it is more than just who you know. Be inspired and inspire. That is how we change the dumbed down culture around us. We choose; we choose to not be dumbed down. We choose to do the hard thing.

We "choose." Sometimes we do not realize we have a choice. It isn't necessarily choosing right or wrong, good or bad; but good or best.

One day an evil hawk snuck up to an eagle's nest and stole an egg. He hid the egg in the nest of a chicken hawk. The hen didn't notice the egg mixed in with her own. When the time came all the eggs hatched. Though he looked different they treated him the same. He would scratch the dirt like them and would try to cluck. Day in and day out he would continually morph into a chicken hawk. He would cluck, scratch and waddle around like one. For, he had become one. One day as he was out again aimlessly scratching away and clucking he looked up into the beautiful blue sky. Beyond the piercing glow of the sun arose an eagle soaring through the heavens. He watched with awe as this majestic, powerful and beautiful commander of the air shot through the blue. He marveled at the piercing eyes, outstretched wings and massive claws. He suggested to the other chicken hawks that they should try to do that; that they too should flap their wings and glide through the air like the eagle. The other chicken hawks looked at him. They looked at the eagle. They looked at each other and then back to him. They laughed. Silly chicken hawk! We can't do that! YOU, can't do that! This eagle, who had become like the chicken hawk, sighed, and agreed; believing that they must be right. He went back to scratching the dirt, eating food from the ground; never looking up again.

How many of us are eagles dumped down to the life of a chicken hawk?

My experience is a spiritual one. I wrote in an earlier chapter that I, unfortunately like so many others, drifted away in high school and throughout college. When I had graduated from college I was cynical and skeptical of religion. I questioned and thought it arrogant to think that Jesus was the only way to God; to Heaven. "Jesus said to him,' I am the way, the truth, and the life. No one comes to the Father except through Me.'" – John 14:6. I had slid right into the cultural mind set all around me. As long as I felt I was being decent and nice to others I would certainly go to heaven. I didn't kill anyone or do anything horrific. There are not any absolute truths. Can't do and not do all the bible says, anyway. Besides, what was really important was that I had a job and was going to contribute to society and have fun the rest of the time. It was my life and I was going to live it. Like a chicken hawk. The only thing was that both my wife, girlfriend at the time, and I felt led to go to church. Even still I had been duped into the worldly thinking that had been dominating my life for the last few years. As I stated, I was very cynical and skeptical. I had been blinded from the truth that I knew earlier in my life. I would go to church, listen, shook my head.

One night my life changed. Even though I had a worldly attitude I was going to pray. As I prayed I still had that cynicism and skepticism in my heart. And, as I have found out, that is where God goes. I was praying and thinking about things the pastor said that I didn't agree with. Never in my life had I felt the conviction that came over me. The God of the universe came in and spoke ever so quietly, ever so loud, in the depths of my being. He is who He is. The Bible is His Truth. It isn't about religion. It isn't about denomination. It is about His Son Jesus. If I would seek Him and put the beliefs of the world aside, I would learn to soar like an eagle.
Choosing to follow Him, being an eagle, is so much harder than living like a chicken hawk. The reward, though, far outweighs the sacrifice. Eternally. God had opened His Word and exposed me to truth. He created me for purposes greater than I would actualize with a world mentality. Through the power of the Holy Spirit I have experienced such fulfillment in the mist of trials of life. I am empowered to live His life of excellence for and through me.

So, are you soaring like an eagle?

CHAPTER 10

Sun – Wind

Oakhurst School, 1st grade, Miss Mika's class.

Here I learned a great lesson that I carry with me to this day. We put on skits, of parables we learned to work on our reading, for kindergarteners. I was part of a parable about the sun and the wind. It made such an impression on me that I remember all of the details of preparation and the performance itself. So much that 34 years later I use this parable for illustration in my public speaking.

It was a cold and windy day where the wind saw a man walking briskly down the street. Though it was cold the man's jacket was not buttoned up. The wind, in his arrogance, smirked to the sun that he was so strong that he could blow the jacket right off the man who was walking down the street. The sun didn't respond. The prideful wind turned toward the man and blew a hard wind at the man. The jacket blew wide open. The man immediately grabbed the two sides of his jacket and pulled it tight. The wind blew even harder. Now, the man on the street used all his strength to keep the jacket tight and to button up. As the wind relentlessly blew the man was determined to get his jacket buttoned up to the top to keep as warm as possible against the cold blowing wind. The man on the road prevailed. He fought off the wind and secured his jacket on himself. The wind blew itself out. The wind was worn out and unsuccessful at his attempt to get the jacket off the man.

Still the sun didn't respond. The wind looked at the sun and said that there was no way the sun could get the jacket off the man. For if he, the wind, couldn't do it that there isn't any way the sun could. He was the powerful wind. The wind, though, did challenge the sun to try. So, the sun, with all his brightness stepped out. And he shined. Feeling the very inviting warmth, the man on the street voluntarily, with a smile on his face, took off his jacket.

Are you the wind or the sun?

Do you shove it down someone's throat? Or do you show kindness and patience; do you yield, allow and listen?

Must you be right at all costs?

Must someone see it your way without giving them a chance to speak/show their view point?

Honestly, I would have to say I have been both. Unfortunately, at times, I have been the wind; trying to force someone to see my way or do something my way.

Sometimes we can be the wind when we "feel" someone should be doing better or different. Earlier in the book I spoke of my daughter Arianna running a 5K with the Girls on the Run. This past May I got to run with my middle daughter Lilli. Lilli had been attending the Girls on the Run sessions twice a week for a couple of months. She has been doing very well and I was excited when she asked me to run with her. As we started off I immediately was trying to encourage her along. After a while she said her foot hurt and she stopped running. I challenged her to keep on going. She started again and then would stop. Instead of encouraging her I began to get pushy. Like the wind on her face she turned away. I was telling her that she worked so hard. She could do it. Come on, come on. She had practiced all this time. I began to irritate her and made her sad. I realized that I was being like the wind and I needed to shine on her. I began to just walk with her. I stayed at her pace not trying to get her to stay at mine. I told her how proud I was of her and that I loved her. After a while, on her own, she began to run again. As we came down the last stretch all the people on the sides of the street were cheering. As with all the runners, they were also cheering for her. She was inspired and finished strong. After the race I realized that I showed both the wind and the sun. When I was the sun was when she did her best.

At times we can become the wind because we are uncertain of ourselves. The most insecure person is the one who has to work so hard in convincing someone because they need convincing too. In this story the wind is like a bully. A bully is a bully because of insecurity in their own lives. Why was it important for the wind to challenge the sun when the sun was minding its own business? What satisfaction was the wind going to get? The wind was out to prove that it had value. That he could do something. He needed the sun's approval. In trying to do so he was humbled.

> "God resists the proud, But gives grace to the humble. Therefore humble yourselves under the mighty hand of God, that He may exalt you in due time." – 1 Peter 5:5b-6

I believe humility comes with knowing who you are. When you know who you are, you know who you are not. If you are clear on that you possess quiet confidence. The tragedy of most comedians, they will tell you, is that they acted out and were comedic to gain approval. You often hear one say that they were so unsure of themselves; insecure. Unfortunately, we are assaulted by media with whom we should be; who we need to be. We end up believing we should be someone that we are not in order to be happy; successful, cool, liked. We grow up wanting to be what was hip. Whatever was the new cool. We so often use the word "wish." I wish I was_____. You fill in the blank. As I have grown in my identity in Christ I have become more and more comfortable with whom I am. It allows me to walk away from what I am not. What happens is we start comparing ourselves to others. We check out to see what someone has and try to match or one up them. When we compare ourselves to others we are giving ourselves a false perception. We start allowing our identity to be what we want others to believe we are. And because it isn't truly who we are, we will be like the wind to convince others. Listen to what Jesus says when the established religious leaders of His day continued to try to discredit Him; to bring doubt.

> "For I know where I came from and where I am going" – John 8:14

Jesus, without a doubt, is fully secure in who He is and doesn't force Himself on anyone. He lives His life; He speaks His truths, and allows the individual to make their choice about who He is. He isn't ever the wind. He is the Son.

Jesus calls Himself the Good Shepherd. A shepherd is familiar with his flock. They know him and trust him. The flock follows the shepherd because their confidence is in him. The shepherd leads and the flock faithfully follows. The shepherd doesn't have to cajole and force the flock. It is a relationship based on trust.

A shepherd isn't exactly what our culture would define as a "real, strong" man. No, we see the cowboy as the tough admirable man's man. The cowboy is the icon of the strong independent America. The cowboy rounded up the herd. There isn't time to build trust. The cowboy isn't there to make nice. He had a job to do and he was going to do it. He isn't worrying about feelings; moving the herd is the only focus. The cowboy would get behind the herd and push. Round 'em up and force them forward. Unfortunately, we tend to assimilate those same characteristics in ourselves.

The shepherd is the example of the sun. He radiates and is embraced and leads. The cowboy is the example of the wind. He forces and manipulates. This is not a knock on the profession of a cowboy who does what he does out of necessity. However, the attitude outside the profession is what brings problems. We can so much get caught up in trends and behaviors that we can miss the adverse affects we can have on others and ourselves.

Is there times when being the cowboy is a necessity; absolutely, as a parent, an employer. What I have found, as both, is that when you make it a habit you are actually having less and less of an impact that's long lasting. Being like the sun is long lasting. In the movie Gladiator, General Maximus, played by Russell Crowe, was respected and his men trusted him. He led and they followed. The king's son, Commodus; played by Joaquin Pheonix, used fear and power. But when it came down to it, the soldier's inevitably showed their allegiance to Maximus. Ultimately, people will allow the shepherd to be the one they will put their trust in. He will be true. He will put them ahead of him/herself. And, they know it.

A sun-like person is a listener
Is patient
Is humble
Yields
Interrupts negativity by being uplifting,
complimentary and encouraging

There is enough wind out there. Be the sun for someone. People are tired of being windswept. Bring light to someone by being sun-like.

THE Son calls you to trust Him; to follow Him. He has put you before Himself. Cursed on a cross he took the full wrath of God that you wouldn't have to. He listens. He is patient. He yields. He uplifts the humble. He is the Good Shepherd. Will you follow?

JULIE'S STORY OF FAITH

Maybe it is a phone call in the middle of the night. Or perhaps a face to face during the middle of the day with words uttered that no one person can take in without their life flashing before them and a feeling that permeates and takes hold of the total being. This is a feeling that no one can empathize with unless they too had those words directed to them. You have cancer. For Julie Thompson, it was even more personal than that when her and her husband Kevin sat in front of Dr. Scott who gave them the results of her biopsy from a lump that she discovered in her breast. Dr. Scott looked at both of them and gently broke the news that she had Invasive Ductal Carcinoma. Julie had cancer.

It was a day like no other day in her life. Truly a day when what she believed her faith to be would be put to the fire.

Joshua was a champion for God. He was faithful in believing God's promise that the Hebrew people could possess the land flowing with milk and honey. He was patient and trustworthy as Moses' assistant and he was a warrior for God in leading God's people to defeat those who were occupying the promised land. When Joshua addressed the people one last time he looked over the vast people and left them with this choice. "Choose for yourselves this day whom you will serve...But for me and my house, we will serve the LORD." – Joshua 24:15

Choosing this day. Everyday we are given a choice. Every circumstance and situation, we have free choice. Make no mistake about it, everyday there is a choice each of us makes. If you wake up and don't think about what I am saying, you still are making a choice. Living a life of excellence is a choice. Your choice is whether your going to serve yourself or your God. Serve your appetite or a bigger cause. Make sure you get yours or make sure others get theirs. Satisfy flesh or satisfy The Spirit. I believe that everyday God has a plan for you. I also believe so does the enemy. Just look at John 10:10. "The thief does not come except to steal, and kill, and to destroy. I have come that they may have life, and that they may have it more abundantly." Think about that. Joshua tells the people to choose. They are to make a deliberate conscious choice. Because the two are on the extreme differing ends, two different end results.

Julie, just like any of us goes about her day, week, month with a full calendar of doing, going, being. As an 8th grade Algebra and science teacher, as well as her middle school athletic director, Julie was always planning one step ahead. Filling out calendar for teams, being in classrooms with dozens of alive and hormone exploding budding teenagers, she needed all the energy she could possibly muster. Each day the energy to keep her schedule was her focus. On top of that she was a mom to two teenage boys and a wife with a home to keep. So, you can imagine that her time was very precious and that nothing was allowed to get in the way of the demands that life had put on her. Life, is there every day, and doesn't wait on anyone. There are so many people that depend on us each day. Our family's first and foremost. As those we work with, work for, and for Julie and so many others, children in classrooms that depend on them.

Julie is a Christian. Her faith is in God through her professed savior Jesus. As a Christian she wants to do and be who God would have her be. In all of that there is the one thing that God wants from all that believe in Him is a relationship. The things we do are great because it shines God on others. However, God desires an intimate relationship with Him. And in that God will allow even the hardest of circumstances to draw us closer to Him; to depend on Him more, to depend on Him and Him alone. Even with Him allowing a lump to form in her breast. I write that last couple of sentences very carefully. Romans 8:28 says, "And we know that all things work together for good to those who love God, to those who are the called according to His purpose." A more accurate translation is that "God works all things". When you first read what I wrote, many people would question a God that gives someone cancer. God doesn't give her cancer. Very important to understand this world being full of sin brings disease, illness, hurts, pains, and ugliness of this world. God allows it, to triumph over it, that others would be drawn to Him. The disciples asked Jesus about a blind man. They wanted to know if it was the man that sinned or his parents that caused him to be blind. "Jesus answered, "Neither this man nor his parents sinned, but that the works of God should be revealed in him." John 9:3. We live in a world that has been afflicted ever since sin entered. God says that, though you are in the world, you are not of it. Since you are in the world you are exposed to ills of the world. God allowing anything to happen to a son or daughter of His is that through trials and tribulation our faith will bring others to salvation. Romans 8:28 should be read not alone but with verse 29. "For whom He foreknew, He also predestined to be conformed to the image of His Son…" The Son suffered. "Though He was a Son, yet He learned obedience by the things which He suffered." – Hebrews 5:8

What Julie thought her faith to be, and what it actually was, were indeed the same.

However, at the same time, how can it be? Not until you are faced with something that is bigger than you, something that can bring an end to your physical life. How can you know how strong your faith really is? How can we ever get to such a deep reverence of God; His grace and mercy, His power and sovereignty, our dependence on Him in the face of our own immortality?

Julie had a choice to make. The choice she made had to be predicated on daily choices that she has made days, weeks, months and years before. She had built her choice on the choice to each day make God her life. His living word is her guide. His commandments are her rule. She built a foundation on the rock. Each one of us, each day, adds to the foundation of our lives that we are building on. Some put their trust and faith in money and the things money can get for us. Our job, the stock market, our investments become the foundation which we build our lives on. It is what we put most of our time and energy into. It becomes our belief for each day that it is our stability, our God. For some it is things of this world.

For Julie Thompson it is her God. El Shaddai, God Almighty, all sufficient one. She put her faith and trust in the living word of God. The Bible would be her truth for He is truth. And it was this faith in Him that she has cultivated to where it would be solid enough when the storm would come.

"Therefore whoever hears these sayings of Mine, and does them, I will liken him to a wise man who built his house on the rock: and the rain descended, the floods came, and the winds blew and beat on that house; and it did not fall, for it was founded on the rock. But everyone who hears these sayings of Mine, and does not do them, will be like a foolish man who built his house on the sand: and the rain descended, the floods came, and the winds blew and beat on that house; and it fell. And great was its fall." – Matthew 7:24-27

What Julie has to say: "The battle in front of me belonged to the Lord. I used several strategies to help me get through this crisis. First, I spoke God's Word and His promises as often as I could."

"For the word of God is living and powerful, and sharper than any two-edged sword, piercing even to the division of soul and spirit, and of joints and marrow, and is a discerner of the thoughts and intents of the heart." – Hebrews 4:12

"Jesus answered and said to them, "You are mistaken, not knowing the scriptures nor the power of God." – Matthew 22:29

As a believer in Jesus as the son of God who died for her sins, rose again that she would have power over sin and the Holy Spirit who enables her to be victorious, Julie has chosen to believe that in Him she has His peace. A peace described in Philippians 4:7 and John 16:33 as not of this world but from God Himself. I myself have just been overwhelmed with His peace "that surpasses all understanding." Julie had built the foundation of her very being on the word of God. That foundation was tested very heavily. The foundation built on the Rock, Christ Jesus, is built on His truths and promises and they were her focus, not her feelings or emotions. The promises of provision, peace and healing were her focus not the circumstance.

> "…and by His stripes we are healed."
> – Isaiah 53:5b.

This verse was one that Julie held on tight to.

She spoke it "in my personal prayer time, my devotion time with my boys, and basically anytime I needed that reminder. I spoke it out loud whenever a friend or acquaintance approached me and talked to me about having cancer. This verse reminded me that Jesus suffered tremendously to heal all of the infirmities known to man. Every stripe He took was a stripe for disease and sin. It not only encouraged me but it served to encourage others."

Before we go any further I feel obligated to add one important note about the preceding verse. Anyone reading this book has had someone that they have loved who had strong faith and have died from the cancer. Don't mistake faith in her healing as arrogance. Julie focused on the truth of His word. But we are to know that God is infinitely wiser than us and that His ways are higher than our ways and His thoughts higher than our own. We are to "trust in the Lord with all your heart and lean not on your own understanding." – Proverbs 3:5. Julie's belief is in that God is sovereign and He will heal her. It is the when and how that she didn't know. Her faith is in Him no matter what. Take this scripture in Daniel as an example:

> "Shadrach, Meshach, and Abed-Nego answered and said to the king, O Nebuchadnezzar, we have no need to answer you in this matter. If that is the case, our God whom we serve is able to deliver us from the burning fiery furnace, and He will deliver us from your hand, O king. But if not, let it be known to you, O king, that we do not serve your gods, nor will we worship the gold image which you have set up." – Daniel 3:16-18

"I had a win-win mentality," Julie says, "If God chose to heal me I win. If He chose to bring me home, I still win. Either way I win."

From there on out she chose to adopt a positive attitude "regardless of what the doctor said to me good or bad." Julie made a choice, based on the empowerment of her belief in His living word that she was going to live a life of excellence no matter how long or short that life was going to be. She was going to live no matter the circumstance, feelings or emotions that she would experience throughout her treatments.

Julie says," I took command of my words and especially my thought life."

Living a life of excellence is the harder choice. It goes against our self centered, self preserving selfish nature. Truly living a life of excellence is one that uplifts others. Julie has been such an inspiration to others including me. I asked her to write for this book because of how much of an impact she had on me when I would see her with her bandana around her head smiling away.

"I blogged my journey on a website called CarePages. Carepages is a wonderful way to keep everyone connected to what was happening to me. I would post updates every time I had a doctor visit or when I had a procedure."

What strikes me here is how Julie exposed herself to others and let them share in her ordeal. Now, cancer was hers and hers alone. However, she allowed everyone into the healing process. By giving specifics Julie was giving her prayer warriors direction to their prayers.

"The effective, fervent prayer of a righteous man avails much." – James 5:16c

Another strategy Julie used was being in fellowship with other believers.

"I joined a Bible study even though there were lots of interruptions with surgery and chemo. I was so thirsty for Him that I studied on my own even though I couldn't always attend. I honestly believed that God slowed me down deliberately to give me this opportunity. I was so busy all the time that I had to find time to squeeze Him into my day. Going through a double mastectomy and chemotherapy offered me ample time to just sit and rest in Him. Something I would never had time to do. He showed me what it meant to fellowship with Him. He took me deeper than I've ever been before."

Unfortunately a lot of times we don't feel we should burden others with our problems, trials, difficulties. We are called to carry each other's burdens and that we ought to pray for one another. We cannot do that if we hide our condition. Sometimes it is a matter of pride. It can be a number of things that keep us from those who are the ones who can fellowship up with us and uplift us.

> "Let each of you look out not only for his own interests, but also for the interests of others." – Philippians 2:4

It is so important to see how we respond to circumstances and situations that we experience in life. How we respond is a gauge of how strong our faith truly is. What is so inspiring to me about Julie is that she responded as a champion of God.

Julie says, "that I do remember writing in my journal in 2006 boldly asking and begging God at times for a change in my relationship with Him. I desperately wanted a deeper fellowship with God and wasn't sure how to get there. I felt at that time in my walk with Him I was so stagnant. I just knew I wanted to be at a different depth with Him. Personally, I believe in my heart of hearts God answered my prayers in 2006 with a cancer diagnosis."

"Trust in the Lord with all your heart,
And lean not on your own understanding"
– Proverbs 3:5

Julie's courage, through her faith, allowed her the Godly wisdom to see through God's eyes. Julie, by way of the Holy Spirit's counsel, was able to see that through this incredible situation was God able to bring her to such an intimate relationship with Him that with all the worldly demands she had been unable to attain. Truth is that God doesn't allow anything to happen if He can't use for the purpose to glorify Himself through it. Not only did it make Julie "be still" that He would draw her closer to Himself but also it was an inspiration to many.

Julie is absolutely correct. It's a win-win situation; a win-win for each of us that have been exposed by her living a life of excellence.

CHAPTER 12

VISION QUEST

"And we know that all things work together
for good to those who love God, to those
who are called according to His purpose."
– Romans 8:28

"You have to have faith that there is a reason
you go through certain things. I can't say
that I'm glad to go through pain, but in a
way one must in order to gain courage and
really feel joy." – Carol Burnett

Jimmy Joe.

Uncommon. Jimmy Joe was uncommon right from
the start; his name. It isn't common on the Jersey Shore
to go by your first and middle name. I have cousins in
North Carolina, where I now live, who are called by
their first and middle name. Robyn Ann, Connie Sue,
even John Boy didn't bring any attention. On the Shore,
though, it certainly was uncommon. Jimmy Joe and I
have been friends our entire lives. Well, almost our entire
lives. I remember the first time I ever saw him. Ocean
Township little league baseball, Colt's Field. I was leaning
against the fence behind home plate of the pee wee field

when strode to the plate, one James Joseph. He looked like Tanner from the Bad News Bears. He wheeled his bat around a dozen times as he got into the batter's box. Twice as many times he scratched the dirt away behind him and three times as many spitting aimlessly. As if he was daring the pitcher to pitch to him. "Who is this cat?" "And who does he think he is?" Man, I'm telling you, he was a character. We were both 8 years old. We lived near each other but went to different elementary schools; therefore I had not met him before. For someone to make such an indelible impression, that is vivid in my mind 30 years later, must be different. Uncommon.

Jimmy Joe was, to my earliest recollection, the first person that stood out from all others around me. He was different. He was uncommon.

I would sit on Jimmy Joe's couch some days after school while his older brother Todd (he has three older brothers; John, Drake, and Todd. All go by their first name only, as everyone else on the Jersey Shore, except Jimmy Joe) would beat the tar out of Jimmy Joe. Not that Jimmy Joe didn't put up a fight. He scrapped. Got tossed around the house, into wall after wall, a few times, but he never gave up. I would sit trying to be still as if the lion was done killing one prey and its attention might be drawn to me if I made a noise or moved. After a while I knew it was safe since we weren't related. I would lounge on the couch waiting for the beating to end so that we can get on with the rest of the day. A friend of ours, John Wolfson, would come in the house. This was our basic dialogue.

John: "What's up Trep?"
Me: "Nothin'"
John: "where's Jimmy Joe?"
Me: "Todd Is giving him a beating"
John: "So, what's you watching?"

Most of us don't want to deal with confrontation especially when it's unsolicited. Even though Jimmy Joe always knew that he was going to get the brunt of the working end, he wouldn't walk away. He would dig in and stand his ground. I wasn't that tough. I was the more common. If I was Jimmy Joe I would have been a yes sir man. Wash your car, Todd? Yes sir. Clean up your room? Yes sir. No more beatings then? Yes sir. Why does the common man compromise? It could be the anticipated pain that will come with standing up for one's beliefs.

Why do I tell you this? Is it to embarrass Jimmy Joe? No, it is quite on the contrary. Whether he deserved it or not (Let it be said, I am sure Jimmy Joe might of deserved some of his beat downs and Todd wasn't some monster.) Jimmy Joe showed in this season of his life how he would deal with unfavorable circumstances and situations, whether they were fair or not. He can look back and see how he gained resolve and determination to deal with everyday challenges. A muscle doesn't grow stronger unless it is tested through resistance.

Jimmy Joe will tell you that though his brothers were a source of frustration, they were instrumental with his successes in wrestling. Wrestling helped him develop important qualities such as self esteem, sportsmanship, work ethic and leadership skills. The bridge of this character growth can be attributed to how he saw himself in the light of dealing with older, aggressive brothers, especially Todd. A very important thought of mine as I look back on those days is that Jimmy Joe never asked for help. I have no shame to tell you that he wasn't about to get it from me. I am not saying there isn't ever a time that you need to ask for help because I believe interdependence overall is stronger than independence. But is only when first independently solid. He didn't ask for help and he didn't make excuses. He did with what he had where he was. Through this he became resolute, determined to face obstacles head on. This enabled Jimmy Joe to be as successful as he possibly could wrestling in high school which undoubtedly leads him in a life of excellence today. One on one with an adversary, that could be stronger and faster, forced him to focus on utilizing all that he was given, mind and body.

This might sound crazy, but his bouts with his brothers, taught him how to focus. Think about it. Here is his older brother coming at him in the confines of the hallway or bedroom. He must pay close attention to how he is coming at him; the areas of escape and what to do for self preservation.

I remember, one day, realizing that, you know what? Jimmy Joe is a pretty good wrestler. It might sound corny, but I was proud of him. During the season Jimmy had to focus and put aside distractions, especially temptations to fattening foods, to keep his weight down while staying as strong as he could. He wouldn't be tempted to stay out late or do foolish things that would compromise the task that was ahead; to be the very best wrestler he could be. He didn't want to cheat himself.

"Let us lay aside every weight, and the sin
which so easily ensnares us, and let us run
with endurance the race that is set before us,
looking unto Jesus, the author and finisher
of our faith" – Hebrews 12:1b-2a

He was willing to make the sacrifices that so many
aren't willing to do. He was willing to be self disciplined
which builds character. The biggest and the hardest
stepping stone to actualizing a life of excellence is
personal discipline.

Jimmy Joe, like all of us, could try to pull the "out"
card. God get me out of this. If you really are there you
would get me "out" of this. God, make Todd go away.
God allows these inconveniences in our life because
he knows what it can cultivate in us in the long run.
Development over deliverance. Don't think with such
trial and tribulation that God will take you out of it.
However He will see you through it for purposes that at
times we may never fully grasp. Look at the life of Joseph.
(Genesis 37-45) He had every reason to pull the "out"
card. God wouldn't have anything to do with it. God
stretched him to reveal his character and in turn be used
by God in such a powerful and empowering way.

"But as for you, you meant evil against
me, but God meant it for good"
– Genesis 50:20a

"No discipline is enjoyable while it is
happening—it's painful! But afterward
there will be a peaceful harvest of right

living for those who are trained in this way." — Hebrews 12:11 Tyndale, New Living Translation

I always thought highly of Jimmy Joe when he would abstain from eating junk food when we were all chowing down on foods like pizza. He kept himself from outside influences that would hinder his ability to go into every match at the highest level, mind and body, that he could. That resolute, determination I spoke of helps one stay clear to stay the course when it would be easy to allow instant gratifications of the flesh overcome you and compromise the goal. The pain of discipline weighs ounces where the regret weighs pounds. That takes deliberates. As I defined earlier, the conscious actions that becomes habits. They are those things that his flesh rebels against because they are inconvenient and because they are hard. It became part of Jimmy Joe's lifestyle. He did it because he had to, regardless of how he felt. That deliberate became a habit out of necessity dealing with his brothers. Todd didn't lay off Jimmy Joe because Jimmy was "having a bad day" or because Jimmy might not "feel like it". Nor because Jimmy was "tired" or "whatever".

Those "whatevers" are those things we don't feel like doing.

Those "whatevers" are because of other people.

Feelings.

Circumstances.

Situations.

Time restraints.

Emotions.

You will always have "whatevers" that you will convince yourself not to do. Keep you from bringing forth the true excellence, true achievement that God has predestined you to. That is exactly what the adversary, the devil, wants you to do. To look and see and think why you shouldn't. Why you shouldn't be deliberate. Jimmy Joe found something out about himself on those high school afternoons dealing with fighting off Todd (and to be fair, at an earlier age from his oldest brothers who by now were out of the house). He was strong. He was resourceful. His best was better than he knew because it had to come out in those situations. And he had the will to overcome regardless of how big the obstacle. That set him up to believe that he could…whatever he was focused on achieving. That allowed him to sacrifice the self satisfaction of giving in to temptation because he could see the more gratifying reward of achievement that waited with discipline and sacrifice. He certainly found out a lot about himself that was bare in front of everyone when he wrestled; one on one- nowhere to hide, no one else to blame. All the hard work, sacrifice and discipline were exposed in those 9 minutes of every match, which is for all to see, all day, every day now.

As Jimmy Joe says himself," There are certain feelings that take place when you wrestle. There can be the feeling of not being successful, which can teach you how to overcome adversity and there is the feeling of winning. It only takes winning once to know the feeling and you'll want to strive to push yourself to be the best you can be. It taught me and others lessons of life."

A young boy in Sparta, Greece, in the days of warriors, was born to be a warrior, a Spartan. In order for him to become a man he was going to have to prove his mettle. He would only be able to do this by standing on his own without a crutch from his parents or friends. Pain was inflicted and the boy would have to defend himself. He would learn to be resourceful and come to know the fortitude that is within him. From the trial he would grow and sense the empowerment that is within that only can come out when the limits of comfort and convenience are forced away and he must find a way to survive. How else would he be able to face adversity and succeed if he had not already been hardened with experience? A tree that stands out on its own and faces the brutal elements will be hardened and strengthened to withstand the storms that would come. A tree that is in the middle of the forest is continually guarded by all the trees that surround it and protect it from the winds and the elements. Though that tree is safe it would not be able to stand alone. It would not have to grow thick with deep strong roots. Iron cannot be sharp without it being grinded on the wheel.

Jimmy Joe made the unconscious decision to face Todd head on and not retreat knowing that it would include pain. He became solid. That is a stepping stone to living a life of excellence. When you stand firm on your core beliefs regardless of what the opposition might say or do. Regardless of which way the wind of popular opinion is blowing, you grow to be solid. Because Jimmy Joe faced adversity in his life then, he now makes a conscious decision to see problems and troubles as challenges. Challenges as opportunities; an opportunity to strive forward and be victorious. Jimmy Joe lives a life of excellence, not because he is married with two children, and has a good job. Actually, they are a great blessing as a result. He lives it because it was chiseled out yesterday for today, tomorrow and beyond.

When it could have been easier to compromise and lower standards using feelings, emotions, situations, circumstances and other people; Jimmy Joe chose to live a life of excellence.

Going back to the beginning of this chapter I have a scripture that is very much used. (Romans 8:28) Many people know this scripture and quote it. But, I believe, it is also misused. From what I have learned is that it isn't God causing the struggles, tribulations, that we go through. There is all of this and more because our world that we live in is farther and far the away from its original design. Because of sin there is so much turmoil, so much injustice, that we now live in a world that has bore the irreparable consequences of what sin has wrought. Here is the good news. God allows it because He will take and mold you. Take the anger and pain and build you, strengthen you. Through all the experiences one goes through He uses it to make you a more polished finished product. His "purpose" is found in verse 29. It is His will that you conform into the image of His Son and to be able to face the driving wind of evil and forgive. It is allowed that you can be able to stand in the shadow of tyranny and praise God. Look at Job. Jeremiah. God knows He made you to be victorious, and through everything He wants you to come to the realization also. He wants you to shine. He wants to show you off. Jimmy Joe came to that point and he is now tougher than he would ever been if he didn't stand before the force before him. He couldn't be as confident and assured through life's twists and turns and up and downs. Jimmy realizes that. That enables him to strive forward, regardless, to strive as a champion.

> "Therefore we do not lose heart. Even though our outward man is perishing, yet the inward man is being renewed day by day. For our light affliction, which is but for a moment, is working for us a far more exceeding and eternal weight of glory, while we do not look at the things which are seen, but at the things which are not seen. For the things which are seen are temporary, but the things which are not seen are eternal." – 2 Corinthians 4:16-18

We must endure hard things; hard circumstances, situations, people. How many times do we ask for God to remove the situation or move us out of it?

I know I have pleaded, whined and cried.

"This is unfair."

"I have done this, this and this…why this?"

"Come on! This is ridiculous!"

"You have gotta be kiddin me! Ahhhhhhhh!!!!!"

Feel free to add any I missed.

On top of that have you ever said, "OK God I understand, I got it. I'm good....OK, I learned, please let me have/take away…"

And then sometimes the situation might seem that it is getting worse!

As Jimmy Joe, those in the Bible, you and me, might think that God is absent or even playing games. I sure have felt that way. The deeper I have gotten with the Word of God the deeper the meditation and closer I become to Him. The closer I have become the more clarity I receive. Now, not that I understand God completely, but I understand His character more which helps me understand, in general, why God allows me to go through. The more I meditate on scripture like the one just above, the more I see that God is at work. It will bring me through victorious if I trust Him to steer me through. What it does is allow me to grow more confident in Him and in Him through me. For what? That He can use me to empathize with someone else who is going through something similar. It is one thing to sympathize with someone through their adversities, hurts and pains, but so much more when we have experienced the same thing. Why did Jesus come? To save the Lost and to know our infirmities that He can empathize with us. Have compassion for us. And intercede on our behalf. Listen, sin has really messed up this world. But God says :

> "He who is in you is greater than he of this world" – 1 John 4:4

He allows you to be affected by the mess of this world and won't take you out of it that you can have an effect on others. This is how His Kingdom advances. One that isn't of flesh and bone but a spiritual one that is greater and everlasting.

God wants you to be a champion. But it has to be for His glory.

> "Let your light so shine before men, that they may see your good works and glorify your Father in heaven"
> – Matthew 5:16

Understanding God's character; the perfect parent, perfect father. I, as a father, am made in His image. I can see the patient process God has with me when I am teaching my girls how to ride a bike after dropping the training wheels. The frustration I see with my girls. They don't understand that it is a process. I know what the outcome will be. I know in the end that they have to go through falling and awkwardness to get the rough edges out before the light bulb goes on. Just as I want to do, when things are tough, they want to retreat and put the training wheels back on. I know that they can't be riding around with training wheels when they are 10. I cannot try to explain to them when they are falling and going nowhere on the bike that they will get through it and the light bulb will go on and they will be so joyous when they take off and are flying free down the street. Going through it doesn't seem light and momentary. But as a father I know it is. I know that they have to do it. With my encouragement, my guidance, my being right there. Though, I can't do it for them. They must do it. But

I am right there. How do I know that they will do it? It is because I am able to empathize with them. I had gone through it as well and persevered and succeeded. Not only can I empathize, just as Jesus can because He experienced what we experience, but like the Holy Spirit, I am right there to guide, comfort, teach and encourage. But in the end she does it and gains confidence in herself for achieving. She also sees, after her crying, frustration and anger, that not only was I right there with her but that I was right. She can do it! That is a stepping stone of living a life of excellence for her. I didn't enable her by allowing her to continue to use training wheels. No, I made her go through and do a hard thing. Now she will be more trusting when the next obstacle comes about because she has this cataloged as a victorious marker in her life.

Know for yourself; see God doing that same with you. He made you. You are in His image. You can do hard things. I know you don't want to. Either do I. Even though I know that it is going to better me, my wife, family, etc. But I trust Him because He is true, He is faithful. No matter how many times my daughter might yell at me, say things she doesn't mean, even though right then and there she says she means it; I am not going to turn on her. We might stop for the day but I will eventually persist because I know that she needs to do it and that she can. But I'm there for her no matter what. He is there for you.

Another point I need to make (I have to give my mother in law credit she mentioned this after she read the aforementioned) is that God's timing is perfect. He knows when and how. God's wisdom is unsearchable.

"Have you not known?
Have you not heard?
The everlasting God, the Lord,
The Creator of all the ends of the earth,
Neither faints nor is weary
His understanding is unsearchable."
– Isaiah 40:28

I wouldn't lead my daughters to learning to ride without training wheels until I believed they were ready. Not until they had been riding with training wheels long enough that it was time. When I look back and see these times in my life, spiritual markers, that I have persevered and got through the more I grow in my faith and trust in God. It is in believing that He allows, that I may grow and achieve. God is perfect. He knows and loves me and is for me not against me. (Romans 8:31)

That is good news.

Clear as mud? Seriously, that simple analogy in my life, God has used to teach me a little about Him and how and why.

Jimmy Joe and Todd. There is not any animosity. They are brothers that care for one another and are in a now different season in their relationship. Jimmy doesn't harbor any resentment. He looks back and sees how it grew him.

Who are the Todd's in your life? How do you see yourself in the midst of it?

How about the Todd's in your life from yesteryear? Have you become stronger because of them or is there some healing, reconciliation needed? For you to move on and live a life of excellence there needs to be.

What are your training wheels?

Can you trust God enough to allow them to come off?

Jimmy Joe has been an inspiration to me all the while we were growing up. I probably never told him and most likely didn't realize it at the time. No matter what, Jimmy Joe never backed down. He always stood his ground and was always one who stood up for the underdog. The world needs more of that inspiration.

CHAPTER 13

FORGIVENESS

"But as for you, you meant evil against me;
but God meant it for good."
– Genesis 50:20

Marlies Treppel. My wife, in her own words.

At the age of 22 I "fell" into a coveted training
program with an international telecommunication
corporation. Fresh out of college, I moved 1,500 miles
away from the only home I ever knew. I was a rural
country girl now on my own to begin life in the big
city with my own money, apartment, and new car. Yet,
something was missing.

I grew up in church. I was there every time the doors
were open. I was saved at the age of six from hell but had
not as an adult intentionally surrendered my life to God.
So, one Friday night I told God I was ready for His plan
for my life. That Sunday evening I was assaulted, raped,
and had my life threatened by a man who apparently had
been stalking me for some time. I thought I was going
to die that night. I had no reason to believe he would
not kill me. I waited for it with blindfolded eyes and
bound hands. Instead, he threatened he would do so if I

ever told anyone. Then, he walked out the door. (I did report the crime. Thanks to a dear friend who came to my frantic call.) The assailant was apprehended 2 ½ years later and was prosecuted for crimes against myself and two other women.

Needless to say, my walk with God was put on hold for quite some time as I dealt with what I perceived to be His answer to my surrender. It seemed to confirm my perception of God. The God of my childhood was cold, punishing and harsh. I was afraid of Him; fearing retribution for every wrong step. He wasn't a God you could have a relationship with.

Wondering how I would live the rest of my life with this I planned a suicide but never made the attempt. Within a year I met Matthew and we married the following year. However, I was basically just surviving. I felt numb yet lived with a mix of fear, anger, sadness, humiliation and hopelessness. I struggled with shame and guilt walking in the shadow of death reliving my nightmare over and over trying to find some purpose, some meaning, and never finding it. I asked myself all kind of questions. What have I done to cause this? These questions turned into statements.

I am a wicked sinner.

I deserve to be brutally victimized and degraded.

I brought this on myself.

I worked in therapy and support groups. I spoke of it when I felt led, knowing it was like releasing poison the more I was able to bring the darkness out in the light. Even from the beginning I was determined to be able to use it to help others.

Spiritually, it took a year from the incident before I spoke to God again. Where was He that night? Why didn't He intervene? I was struggling deeply with this. I needed peace. I went and began meeting with my pastor.

In a few months God began to reveal Himself to me. I slowly began a tenuous relationship of trusting Him. As my walk grew more intimate and my faith and trust increased I was able to get to the root of my hurt, my perceived abandonment of God. Where was He? At last on my knees, crying out, wailing in despair, My Lord comforted me. Several days later I was given more grace than I deserve. God revealed Himself to me. I had been in His hands all the while. I had never left them-even when I thought I had. In my darkest moment he was right there. He was there with me in the ugliest, most vile and humiliating moments of the assault. God Himself was as devastated as I by what happened. However, He knew something I did not at the time. I would be victorious. He knew that I would prevail. Though it grieved Him, He knew that He could use it, leading me into a deeper faith and relationship with Him. Through it I have come to know a different God than my childhood. I met Jesus, the lover of my soul, who takes the nails for me each day. Who wants me to love Him preeminently and be faithful to Him in all things. I have found peace. Real peace. "…that in Me you may have peace. In the world you will have tribulation; but be of good cheer, I have overcome the world." – John 16:33.

He saved my life (both literally and figuratively) that night in so many ways and has now rescued my heart and soul. I see Him there and I am at peace. I have given Him all my hurt and shame. I have named each and every one and said them out loud so they will no longer have power over me. I have left them at the cross. There is hope and I have it. I use the hurt and pain in my life for good-just as He has.

With this critical vertical relationship fully in place I was prepared to be fully free.

Forgiveness is a powerful courageous act initiated by choice and sustained by a trust in something or someone greater than you. For me, that is in my God, the Maker of the Heavens and the Earth, the Creator and Sustainer of life. My God is also the Ancient of Days who sits upon His throne and will judge all in the end. This works both ways, encouraging me to offer mercy and forgiveness. Fully trusting in Him I forgave the prisoner who is serving 18-20 years. At first this was a whisper in my mind as something I needed to do. Then it became a discussion with God. This led to the decision and act of intentionally forgiving. Then it became a supplication for the prisoner's rehabilitation. Finally, it became a letter written and mailed to him fully stating my forgiveness of what he had done to me. What was intended for evil, my God has used, and will continue to use for good. I am free. All that remains are the scars that bring empathy to others who are suffering and/or struggling. It has led to three years in seminary culminating in a Masters degree in Religion focusing in Pastoral Counseling. Only God knows from here.

Is forgiveness easy? No way! But the freedom and peace that is gained is well worth the struggle. Extending forgiveness allows me to no longer be bound. I am delivered, released. I am no longer defined by it. I have overcome by the act of forgiveness. The devil has no power over me as he did after the incident with his lies. I am the daughter of the Most High God who created me for Himself. I spoke, in the first paragraph, of something missing. Something was missing even though I had a job, money, friends, and things. I no longer have anything missing. In Him I have everything and more.

Do all the memories go away? Uh-uh! Just typing this has brought floods of them with tears to match but there is no pain, no fear, and no worry; just indescribable peace. Let me be clear. I do not believe God caused the attack, but I do believe He allowed it for His purpose in my serving in His Kingdom. He knew, as He did with Job in the Old Testament and Peter in the New Testament, that He could allow Satan access to me but I would turn to Him for life.

Does this make me some kind of spiritual giant? Absolutely not! Instead consider Corrie Ten Boom and her forgiveness of a guard, one of the cruelest she remembers, at Ravensbruck concentration camp where she was held captive during World War II. According to the account in the *Guideposts magazine* (1972) he came up to her after she spoke to a church in Munich, Germany on God's forgiveness. She recognized him instantly, though he did not know her. However, even though he had become a Christian this man was thankful to be reminded his sins were forgiven and wanted her forgiveness as a prisoner of Ravensbruck. She had a choice to make—to put action to her message of God's love and forgiveness or forever nurse bitterness and remain paralyzed as she had seen so many do since the war. She prayed for Jesus to help her, lifted her hand accepting his, and God flooded her with healing as she spoke the words of forgiveness to him.

Choosing forgiveness transforms a victim into a victor.

Where is God in the darkest moment of your life?

Where do you need healing?

Where do you need to offer forgiveness?

Where do you need to receive forgiveness?

Do you trust God? Would you take a step of faith to seek Him? He will not fail you. In Him you will find peace. "Ask, and it will be given to you; seek, and you will find; knock, and it will be opened to you." – Matthew 7:7

Marlies Treppel received her Master of Arts in Religion – Pastoral Counseling degree from Liberty Theological Seminary in August 2010.

I would like to add in August 1991 I was leaving my parents house in Carolina Beach, NC to go back to New Jersey. I was leaving to go back to my senior year of football and college. As I left, I told my parents that as much as I loved them I would never live there. I would visit them but I was staying in Jersey. In January 1993 a couple of friends and I shared a house on the Jersey

Shore, when out of nowhere I woke up and told my roomies I was packing up and moving to North Carolina. Marlies and I have researched the days of me inexplicably moving to North Carolina (where Marlies had moved to be with her family) with her incident and concluded that they were within 72 hours of each other.

CHAPTER 14

ARETE'
TO LIVE A LIFE OF EXCELLENCE

Our deepest fear is not that we are inadequate. Our deepest fear is that we are powerful beyond measure. It is our light, not our darkness, that most frightens us. Your playing small does not serve the world. There is nothing enlightened about shrinking so that other people won't feel insecure around you. We are all meant to shine as children do. It's not just in some of us; it is in everyone. And as we let our own light shine, we unconsciously give other people permission to do the same. As we are liberated from our own fear, our presence automatically liberates others. – Movie, *Coach Carter*

CHAPTER 15

PARTING WORDS FROM THE AUTHOR

It has been close to a year that I sat in the parking lot of the Holiday Inn getting set speak to a room full of people for 25 minutes between their lunch and getting back to their exhibits. As I was introduced, I do as I always do before I speak; I thank specific people for the opportunity to share and then before I speak, I pause. I scan the room and look into faces of the people assembled in the room. As I skim across the audience I see some who have a look of "please hurry up and get this over with." Others are fidgety and distracted. And there are some (hopefully) that are looking right back at me with a look of anticipation. As I say with anything I write or speak, my hope is that there might be one thing that someone can take with them that will be a small ingredient that can be part of a their whole make up. Well, this particular day was the same as the others. All three of those examples of people were present.

Most of what I talked about is right here in this book. When I was done I got a chance to talk to a few people who were in the audience. Everything went fine until just about the time I was getting ready to leave. A gentleman came up to me and expressed how much my words spoke to him and it challenged him. It was if I was there just to speak to Him. I thanked him and was glad that it had that affect on him. After I got in my car I thanked God and then reflected.

I knew that when he said that "I" spoke to him it was God through me. I am not adequate. I acknowledged that I have insecurities, things that I cannot overcome; not in my own power. God opened my eyes, that it wasn't about my situations and circumstances. I will always have trials (John 16:33). It is how I am responding within those challenges. I recognizing that enabled me to allow God to speak through me. God is empowered through me in spite of my weaknesses; because of my weaknesses, inadequacies and insecurities.

> "He gives power to the weak,
> And to those who have no might He increases strength." – Isaiah 40:29

> And He said to me, "My grace is sufficient for you, for My strength is made perfect in weakness." – 2 Corinthians 12:9

Living a life of excellence isn't me directly living it because I can't. It is me fully acknowledging that it is His excellence that increases through me as I decrease; as I humble myself in confessing my weaknesses and acknowledging His strength.

> "Therefore humble yourself under the mighty hand of God, that He may exalt you in due time" – 1 Peter 5:6

Going through what we have been going through is nothing but humbling. I also came to realize that I should focus more on development and not deliverance. That in these times of difficulties is when we lean on God even more and He can develop us more into the image of His obedient Son.

I have to confess more and more that "I just don't know". But that is okay. I am not to reason in my own mind why or how God uses situations for a bigger purpose. But, it isn't for me to figure it all out. It is for me to have faith in God that He does. And that I am to trust Him regardless.

> "Trust in the LORD with all your heart,
> And lean not on your own understanding;
> In all your ways acknowledge Him,
> And He shall direct your paths."
> – Proverbs 3:5-6

It was in this scripture that I received the peace of God that passes all understanding that permitted me get in that room in front of people and speak clearly with the message that had an impact if only for that one man.

Living a life of excellence is acknowledging the perfect excellence in the One who created you. He created you unique that no one else in this world is exactly like you. He created you that He may live excellence through you that others would be drawn to that excellence; to Him.

It isn't easy. At times it is hard just to get through a day. I surely have lived more of those days than I would have liked. It is easy to look at someone else and believe that it is easier for them because they have X or that they don't have to deal with Y. It leads me to Jesus telling the parable of the Loaned Money (Matthew 25). There was 3 servants each given different amounts of money. It was not where they started that counted but were they finished. The one with five bags of silver, and two bags, both doubled theirs. They both were commended and were found faithful. They both were had different abilities but used them to the fullest. Yes, some people do have more than you. Some have advantages over you in certain areas. It is, though, what you do with what you have been given, where you are. There was a third servant who received one bag of silver. This servant hid the money and did nothing with it. Each one was given different portions and was expected to cultivate and increase the amount. This third one did not. The little he had was taken away. What we all need to realize that whichever portion we are given isn't even ours. We are stewards of it. We are to manage what we are given that it would increase and be used to the betterment of others. God has blessed each of us with gifts and talents and He wants us to use them to the fullest. The owner of the bags of silver in the parable is God. Reading the parable you will see that God is well pleased with the one who turned 2 into 4, just as the one who had turned 5 into 10. Even though the one with 10 had more than twice as much as the one with 4 God was just as well pleased because they both did the same with what they had been given; they doubled it.

> "His lord said to him, 'Well done, good and
> faithful servant; you have been faithful over
> a few things, I will make you ruler over

many things. Enter into the joy of your
lord.'" – Matthew 25:23

I would hate to think that when I go to Heaven
God will show me all that I missed on Earth because I
wasn't faithful to use all that I was given for His purposes.
Faithful with little, more is given. As I have said, it can be
difficult. But, more the reason to strive through that you
may be a shining light in someone's darkness; a person's
motivation, their hope. God has called each of us to live
a life of excellence, even in the midst of difficulty, that
others may be inspired as well.

It is my prayer that you will find something from
this book that speaks to you and add another ingredient
that God can use to live a life of excellence through you.
You never know who is watching you that you have the
opportunity to bless.

I was at first writing this book with a different theme.
The book was going nowhere and I questioned that I
should even be writing another book. Until, that is, that
May 2009 morning when I was watching my 9 year
old pounding the pavement running the 5K I spoke of
earlier in the Intro chapter. Her face was flushed red with
sweat flowing down the sides of her face. She had such a
focused, serious look on her face. At that moment I was
truly inspired by my daughter. Of course, she had no
idea. To see her running 3.1 miles was so uplifting that
it challenged me to desire to strive and excel. This book
was launched by her achieving and finishing strong that
morning. I couldn't be more proud of her or her sister
Lilli, who I ran with this past May, 2010. I learned an
important, valuable lesson that morning with Lilli, which

I have shared in this book. I do not tell Marlies enough how much I am blessed by what she has overcome and what God has done in her life. Julie, Jimmy Joe and Kim might have never known that they inspired me. We never know. And that is exactly why we are to live a life of excellence. May we fully embrace this life that God has blessed us with and live it in excellence; that we may pass it on.

Thank you for taking the time to read this book. My prayer is that it might lead you to pause and reflect, and encourage you to strive to live a life of excellence.

WEBSITE

To see all that God is doing through Matt helping others live a life of excellence, go to: **www.truelifeabundant.com**

To contact Matt for speaking engagements, email: **mtreppel@gmail.com**

To order more copies of this book or Matt's first book, *Live the Life Abundant,* email: **mtreppel@gmail.com** or visit **www.amazon.com**

CPSIA information can be obtained at www.ICGtesting.com
Printed in the USA
BVOW010331270613

324421BV00009B/74/P